ETCH YOUR NAME IN TIME

31 Principles To Craft a Lasting Legacy

PEARL JOHN

FOREWORD BY KRISH DHANAM

INDIA • SINGAPORE • MALAYSIA

ISBN 979-8-88909-902-4

Credits

Content: Pearls
Cover Page Concept and Design: Ms. Divya John
Proof Reading: Mrs. Priyadarsini John
Publishing: Mr. Shijoy and Notion Press Team

Patron & Sponsor: Mr. Solomon Raj

Scripture References: All scriptures quoted from - the New International Version and the New King James Version unless specified from the Message (MSG) or the Amplified version (AMP).

Dedication

To the greatest legacy builder of all time and all those who strive to build and leave a legacy.

Table of Contents

Foreword

With great joy and a profound sense of honour, I pen these few words in celebration of an incredible collection of leadership principles. The stories, anecdotes, references, and illustrations in the book *Etch Your Name in Time* are prime principles for anyone aspiring to be a person of influence. In addition, my dear friend Dr. Pearl John has brilliantly created practicality in the application from some of the heroes of history.

Reading this book will give you great insight into the life and patriarchy of Abraham and simultaneously allow you to explore the tenets and teaching of Moses. In addition, this book will let you examine King David's faults and flaws to illustrate that one's past can beat or befriend them. And as you are perusing Daniel's patience and perseverance in captivity and exile, a personal leadership fortitude will emerge.

This historical and anecdotal journey through the legacy of individuals and institutions gives a fresh perspective that allows you to etch your name in history. The desired outcome of this book is to change the reader's life and cement their legacy. Dr. Pearl John creates a functional roadmap utilizing his practical leadership success in national and international arenas. The roadmap through the lens of Abraham, David, Daniel, and Moses prepares you to define, develop, and deploy the truth within you.

A great philosopher once said that timeless truths are God's love letter to his children. He added that if any living person does not feel God's love, he or she is probably reading someone else's mail. Thus, through the annals of history, proven and validated truth has been the most significant source of life application and living wisdom. It is an evidential synopsis that has outlived the pallbearers who seek to carry its demise. Use the tenets of this book to run parallel with the wisdom of time-tested teaching to perform and perfect the practice that influences others for years to come.

– Krish Dhanam
Author and Speaker

Preface

At some point in your life, you think about the legacy you leave behind. If you have not thought about it – perhaps this is an opportunity to do so. As I was preparing this message, I asked myself if I was equipped to write on the topic; as I reflect on my life I see there are more opportunities than accomplishments, more gaps than giftings, more issues than innovations and I almost dropped the idea of penning this book.

I believe it was the deep inner prompting that made me review my decision and reconsider my view in the light of the Writ, "I do not consider to have achieved, but I press on towards the goal." Thus, I took courage and thought it useful to bring this perspective, which would aid both young and old to consider this important issue pragmatically. That would completely change the way you think, live, and have your being in this beautiful world.

The issue of legacy has had a great impact on my personal life and has changed me for the better, and I believe all of us would want to leave a positive legacy. History has often scripted the lives of giants whose life stories have had a telling effect across centuries and, in some cases, beyond millenniums. Studying their lives, reviewing their work, and learning from their mistakes should lend credible ways to orchestrate your life and enable you to continue the good you are doing and take corrective steps where course correction is required. The intent of this book is not to 'sermonize' but rather to expound, exhort, and provide options for thought and action. I have taken the liberty of using several examples from my life; my challenges as also what worked well to iterate the lessons that have been drawn.

Having reviewed a range of literature on leadership behaviours and leader effectiveness, I have been deeply touched by the ancient Writ spread across multiple millennia; many of them were ordinary human beings but ended up becoming extraordinary giants of stature rewriting their worlds. Thus, considering the lives of a few of these stalwarts who have left a lasting legacy allows us to examine their lives and draw up key lessons that will aid us in living to leave a legacy.

The book is addressed to leaders – leaders of all genres, particularly those who are so consumed by 'today' that they have fewer energies to focus on 'tomorrow'.

The book unfolds 31 principles – the intent is to pick up a principle a day and go over the entire book in a month, internalizing the principles and applying them. Perhaps revisit this book every quarter so you are re-aligning and making course corrections as appropriate regularly. At the end of each principle, there is space provided for reflection, response, and action. Use this to note your takeaways and action points to track regularly.

There are occasions the narrative transitions to addressing the protagonists in the second person – where the intent is to identify the protagonists with the reader.

May this effort help you craft your legacy and leave an impact on this life and beyond!

– Pearl John
February 2023
Mumbai

Endorsements

Drawing from his rich and diverse experiences in the country and abroad Dr. Pearl John inspires leaders to subscribe to a set of profound leadership principles that form the bedrock of leadership excellence. The principles outlined are so practical, powerful, and propelling, that should any leader of any genre adopt them they will find themselves on the right track to achieving and surpassing their goals and objectives. The format of the book allows for a principle to be focused on in a day and covers the 31 principles in a month with space built in for notes to reflect and respond which makes the book highly actionable with a possibility of revisiting the principles repeatedly until they are ingrained into the leader; both those who take baby steps in the leadership journey and the more mature leaders. Strongly recommended to read, re-read and reap the value this book unlocks.

– Mr. Solomon Raj
Ex Dy.Managing Director of State Bank of India
Ex-Managing Director of IndusInd Bank
Advisor to Hinduja Group

The impactful book *Etch Your Name In Time* by Dr. Pearl John is a powerful exploration of the concept of legacy and its ability to shape the future for generations to come. Written through a combination of in-depth research and personal reflection, the book addresses three groups of people: those who unconsciously set up legacies, those who consciously strive to shape their legacies, and those who are not currently thinking about legacy building. Dr. John encourages readers to focus on the spiritual aspect of legacy building and emphasizes the importance of considering the long-term impact of one's actions. The book also provides designated periods for contemplation, consideration, and cerebration for a healthy mind, and offers insights on how legacies are built over a lifetime. Overall, *Etch Your Name In Time* is a must-read for anyone looking to understand the importance of legacy and how to create a lasting impact.

– Mr. Anand Pillai
Chief Transformation Officer
Leadership Matters Inc.

Dr. Pearl John brings together a rare combination of ancient wisdom, contextual corporate examples, and lessons from his own successful career to highlight the need and means to leave a legacy that matters. My studies indicate that Power, Purpose, Values, and Significance are the four tenets that differentiate the good, bad, and ugly sides of Leadership. This book addresses all four tenets, thereby providing the reader with a strong foundation to become a Servant Leader. So if you desire to be a leader whose name will be etched in time, I strongly encourage you to read it in the recommended manner, one principle a day, reflect on it, respond to the challenge, and identify things that you can do to implement the principle in your life. You will be blessed.

– Dr. Madana Kumar, PhD
Servant Leadership Evangelist and
chief consultant at Leadyne
Author of *Not-So-With-You*

Søren Kierkegaard, a Danish theologian said, "Life can only be understood by looking backwards, but it must be lived looking forward." Dr. Pearl John, in this book, with his penetrating insight, has gleaned from the lives of four leaders of the past and 31 outstanding principles, which would help one build a lasting legacy. In his enunciation of each of these principles, Dr. John brings together theology and practice in amazing harmony. Many of his advocacies are backed by the experiences drawn from his own exemplary life. Each of these 31 inspirational vignettes, gently but surely nudges the reader to the goal. The author has presented in this book 31 principles – nay – 31 precious pearls. Grab and grasp them; don't miss any. I heartily commend this book.

– Mr. Raja B. Singh
Senior Partner – RK Khanna & Associates
International Trustee – Gideons International

Having worked in leadership roles and coached leaders for the best part of the last 30 years, what a treasure to discover Dr. Pearl John's book looking at 31 principles on how to craft a lasting legacy. But this is not for the faint of heart. It is for those who are committed and passionate about not merely wanting to leave their mark on future generations, but for those who want their legacy to count today! For it is only when we model courage, humility, leadership, self-sacrifice, perseverance (and more) today that we can get a glimpse into how those things can change the tomorrow of future generations.

– Mr. Glenn Williams
Chief Executive Officer
"Helping leaders achieve their goals without sacrificing what is important."
LCP Global

Acknowledgement

I am grateful to the Lord Jesus Christ, who predestined, chose, called, and commissioned me to accomplish this task among others. He is the reason for my existence and much of what is captured here are insights gleaned from Him through time.

I express my deep gratitude to my dad, Dr. Arthur John, and mom, Mrs. Lizzie Arthur who modelled a life of building and leaving a legacy, they have played a significant role in shaping me and I owe much of my learning to them.

My thanks to Dr. E Janifer and Mrs. Premila Janifer, my parents-in-law who were instrumental in bringing my wife into my life.

My appreciation for Mrs. Priyadarsini John, who has been my constant companion, consistent supporter, and constructive critic. Without her support, this book will not be.

My heartfelt thanks to our daughter Ms. Divya John, who has been a bundle of joy, and much of what I have written is a legacy that I desire for her to experience and enhance. She also has the distinction of coining the title for this book and designing the cover page.

My deepest gratitude and regards to Mr. Solomon Raj, the Ex-Managing Director of State Bank of India, Ex-Managing Director of Indus Ind bank, and Advisor to the Hinduja Group who saw the potential of this book even before it was formed and encouraged me to put it together, financed the publishing of this book and endorsed the book.

I am deeply indebted to Mr. Krish Dhanam for kindly agreeing to write the foreword, despite his tight schedule. And also Mr. Anand Pillai, Dr. Madana Kumar, Mr. Raja B. Singh, and Mr. Glenn Williams, all of whom have graciously taken time out of their busy schedules to read and endorse the book.

Introduction

A powerful way to wrap up life narratives and project important aspects of identity as experienced and expressed in life stories to future generations is by creating and transmitting a legacy. It gives a sense of purpose from the perspective of the past to the future. Charting a legacy, nurturing it, and treasuring it for posterity is often unconsciously done by many leaders. Others consciously endeavour to shape their legacies such that future generations will learn of, learn from, and learn to live lives that mirror the tenets left behind. There are still others who are so consumed by the here and now that they consciously blind themselves to future considerations.

This book is an attempt to address all three groups mentioned above. The leaders who unconsciously set up legacies for generations to follow, those who consciously strive to shape the legacies they leave behind and take painstaking efforts to ensure they are intentionally creating and sustaining a legacy that will set their stamp on it. This book also addresses the third group who have adopted a more myopic approach to life and are concerned about their daily, weekly, monthly, or yearly targets and are happy meeting them, whose lives revolve around the 'now' and have scant regard for tomorrow. The hope is that the pages herein will enable the unconscious legacy builders to consciously focus on elements that are not concentrated on and the conscious legacy builders to have a re-iteration of the facets they focus on. It is also my desire that those who are not thinking of legacy building, reconsider their stance and focus on building and leaving a legacy.

Designated periods for contemplation, consideration, and cerebration are indispensable for a healthy mind just as exercise, exertion, and effort are an integral part of physical fitness, spiritual fitness is a product of reading, reflecting, and responding to the spiritual element consistent with the demands of the Writ; where the equation accentuates the physical fitness over the mental fitness or the mental fitness over the spiritual, the balance is lost and invariably results in lopsided outcomes. Often the physical and mental sides are focused on as they are the more tangible facets. The spiritual dimension is underplayed and often neglected. However, when required to prioritize, emphasis ought to be given first to spiritual fitness for it transcends the earthly domain and extends into eternity and thus should take pre-eminence. From a legacy-building perspective, the spiritual element takes centre stage for a long-term legacy that spans across the horizon, going beyond generations. Thus, there is a marked emphasis on the hereafter rather than hitherto; while hitherto has been leveraged from the pages of history to shape the lessons detailed herein.

Legacies are not built in a day. They are built in a lifetime; brick by brick, layer by layer, step by step. You reinforce the building blocks until the superstructure is ready. Every leader should take upon himself/herself the task of building a lasting legacy that weathers the test of time and space. As you invest your time and consider your eco-system judiciously and keep a line of sight to the longer term you will not merely build but shape the legacies of many.

Before I unravel the elements that make the legacy real and possible, it is perhaps important to have a shared understanding of what legacy is.

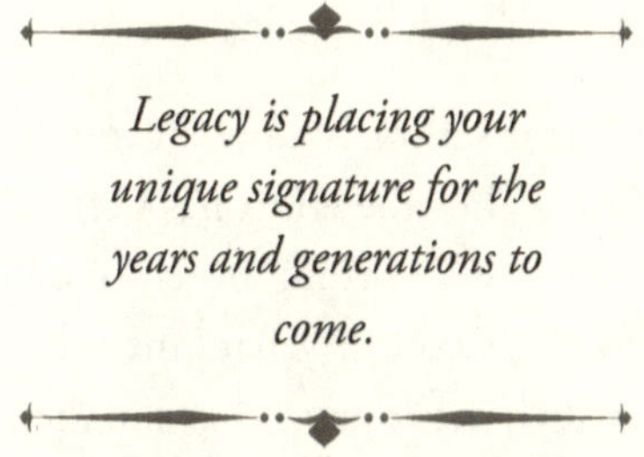

What is a legacy? What does it mean to leave a legacy? Legacy is placing your unique signature for the years and generations to come, whereby you take cognisance of how your actions today will shape tomorrow for posterity. It is an ability to take a view across the horizon and intent to influence the future through your thoughts, words, and actions. This entails an overwhelming concern for the emerging world such that the actions of today will influence and impact the experience of tomorrow. A calligrapher named Prem Behari Narain Raizda handwrote the original Indian constitution. It was never printed. He did this for free; what he desired was his place in history and wanted his name to appear on each page of the document. What an effort at legacy building!

Legacy is not leaving something for people. It is leaving something in people said *Peter Strople.* The greatest legacy one can pass on to one's children and grandchildren is not money or other material things accumulated in one's life, but rather a legacy of character and faith said *Billy Graham.*

When you think of giants that left a legacy, Mahatma Gandhi, Nelson Mandela, Abdul Kalam, and JRD Tata are perhaps pre-eminent. There is something about their lives that leave a lasting impression – an abiding impact and perhaps an enduring influence. While these lives are worthy of study and emulation, I have delved into the past and picked four stalwarts who have changed the course of history and left legacies that have lived for centuries, thus perhaps providing us with a broader canvas and a wider reach to consider.

Wisdom as espoused in the ancient scripts is a potent tool to leverage as it applies to our times. Thus the effort has been to zero in on these exemplary leaders who through their words and actions significantly impact their worlds. What I intend to do is to refer to the context in which they operated in and then deep dive into their lives to draw lessons that may be relevant to our contexts and times.

- I -

Abram Called Abraham, the Amazing Visionary

The renowned patriarch Abraham (c. 20th century BC) is known to have been born in southern Chaldea, most likely in or around the Mesopotamian city of Ur. According to ancient tradition, Abraham (formerly known as Abram) married Sarah (originally known as Sarai), and set off on a protracted journey from Mesopotamia to Haran, and eventually to Canaan and Egypt. Abraham's name ultimately comes to imply "father of a multitude" and/or "the buddy of God", as described in Genesis chapters 12-25. Abraham and Sarah interact with a wide variety of civilizations, customs, and people groupings over their long and dramatic trip as described in the ancient texts.

Abraham is one person who altered history and through whose lineage one of the greatest nations of the world was born! He is undoubtedly the father of the nation of ancient Israel. As you read of Abram, you will soon recognise that he was an ordinary person, just like you and me. So what was it that transformed this ordinary man into a legend that left a legacy for millennia to remember? I outline eight principles that may be gleaned from the life of Abraham and that may be deemed to be common among legacy builders.

PRINCIPLE 1

Be Sensitive to a Call From Beyond

> Genesis 11:28-30 [28]*And Haran died before his father Terah in his native land, in Ur of the Chaldeans.* [29]*Then Abram and Nahor took wives: the name of Abram's wife was Sarai and the name of Nahor's wife, Milcah, the daughter of Haran the father of Milcah and the father of Iscah.* [30]*But Sarai was barren; she had no child.*

Here we find the beginnings of Abram referenced. Abram had taken his wife Sarai and she was barren. He lived in Haran which means parched, he lost his father Terah and was mourning his loss. What a situation to be in! His life was falling apart, his personal world had come crumbling down; he and his family were going through a rough, tough patch – he lived in a parched land, his father died and his wife was barren. His immediate context was not particularly great, his closest relative was no more and his dearest wife was unable to give him the pleasure of being a father; this is adversity at its worst. Adversity has a telling effect; as you go through adversity you turn desolate, despondent, and depressed and you are so self-absorbed and are given to self-pity that you are oblivious to external stimuli or internal nudging. In adversity, he heard a call – a call that compelled him to stop, consider and act!

What was the call?

> We have the call scripted.
>
> Genesis 12:1 *Now the LORD had said to Abram: "Get out of your country, From your family and from your father's house, To a land that I will show you."*

I would like to highlight three key lessons on receiving and responding to the call. The call is a powerful stimulant, it provides a sense of purpose, propels you to action, and presents you with meaning. So how does one get wind of this calling?

a. Tune In To The Right Network

We live in a digital era and are familiar with the workings of a network. For seamless communication, you need to be tuned into the right network; often, when you use the mobile and you don't get to hear the other side you would say, "oh, the network is bad." If you are using the 'A' network and go to a location where the 'B' network is strongest then it is likely that you will not get connected.

You have the highest reception when you have the strongest network. There are occasions you find yourself aligned to the 'A' network but when meandering in an area where the 'B' network is strongest you experience breaks in connectivity.

I want to highlight for you the most strongly established network in the world – it's a soft but sure, surreal but significant, subtle but strong network. There is an integral need to be in sync with the soft voice that comes through strongly in the most unexpected of times. Being open to the calling is a pre-requisite to receiving the calling. Those who are totally opposed to the possibility of the supernatural are often individuals who are unaware of anything outside their temporal, worldly pursuits. They have effectively put a stop to everything that transcends the boundaries of the physical world. When you are overly obsessed with the physical, you run the risk of excluding alternatives that are not related to the physical.

From a longer-horizon perspective, there is a need to be aligned with the right network. Abram was in sync with that network; the right network which gives you inner assurance, internal confidence, and an inmost feeling of security. When he received the call, he was quick to catch it. Have you heard the calling? Have you missed the call? If you have not oriented yourself to hear the calling – perhaps it is about time to incline your ear to do so.

b. Align Your Sensors To The Right Frequency; Don't Let The Disturbances Distract You

The causes for a bad signal fall under two categories: localised poor coverage due to disastrous interference, and the distance from or obstacles between your phone and the nearest cell tower. Alignment to the right frequency is a pre-requisite for a seamless connection. However, distractions invariably infringe on the connection. Distracted driving is among the leading causes of car accidents; higher than reckless drivers who were intoxicated, fast drivers, or those who run a red light. Distracted drivers frequently take their eyes off the road to use a cell phone, send texts, or eat. Distractions are diabolical. Distractions are dangerous. Distractions are death-inducing.

Distractions can come in different forms – long hours being spent on social media, surfing the net, wrong friends who encourage you to waste time on unproductive pursuits, unnecessary preoccupation with smartphones, getting high/ drunk, getting lost in music, being addicted to television/video games among others are potent causes for distractions.

The question is: are you so distracted that you don't catch the signals from beyond? This perhaps is an opportune time to reflect. Abram was not distracted despite legitimate reasons for him to get distracted as we all do. Instead, he aligned his sensors to the right frequency and he caught the right signals. The key to note is that the signals are clear, distinct, and definitive. The question is, do you catch those signals?

c. Alter Your Course In Accordance With The Call Signals

When you catch those signals, you have to continue in the network area for uninterrupted signals. When you receive the signals and the calling is unmistakable, unequivocal, and unambiguous, give heed to the call and alter your course in line with His signals.

When you hear His voice; the expectation is to alter your course: 'Abram, this is the Rock of Ages speaking – Abram, I want you to head out to the country that I will show you.' What do you do? You say, "yes, Lord." It is tough, no doubt. It would mean letting go of your favourite music, it could mean missing your favourite television serials, it could mean jeopardising your favourite pass time or anything that you hold dear. But when the call comes through, you let go and let God!

Simple compliance can work wonders. Where protocols are violated, the consequences are severe. What would have been the consequences if Abram had decided to stay put and not listen to His voice? He would not have crafted a legacy for generations to thrive on.

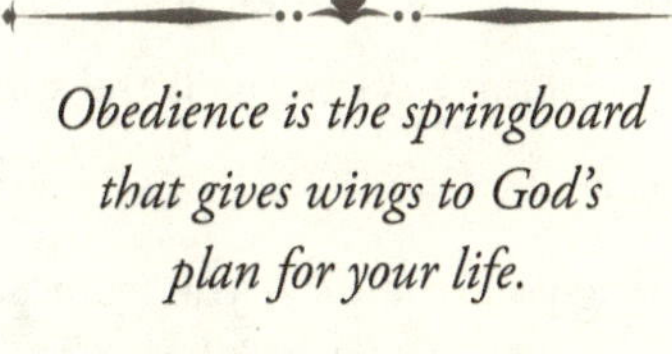

According to a survey, the sixth major cause of car accidents is jumping signals. Obedience is the springboard that gives wings to God's plan for your life. The question is, are you walking in obedience to that inner nudge, the inner voice, that distinctive calling that you have perhaps not paid heed to? How many areas have you explicitly disregarded? This is an opportunity to set that right. When you violate His word, you miss out on a significant part of the legacy. Someone said 'Many pages of your biography are torn away because of disregard for the soft nudging in the inner self.' How true!

Let's assume you are off on a journey from Mumbai to Manali; you have never been to Manali and this is the first time you are venturing out. What would you do? You will get into your car and activate the GPS and proceed as per the directions provided by the GPS. That is essentially what you are called to do! In life's journey, you have a much more potent GPS. Do you know what GPS stands for? Guiding Post Superior. There is a guiding post. You may not recognise it. But when you open yourself to the guiding post and are inclined to the guidance you receive from the guiding post, you shall never be lost! The GPS of life also perhaps can be termed as God

Pointing System; God is the source of direction when you open yourself to Him – He points the way forward.

Did you know 2/3rds of GOD is GO – embedded in the term GOD? That is the heartbeat of GOD; there are many Abrams who hear that distinct voice to GO – that gentle nudge in the spirit that calls you to GO, and you have been resisting. You have generated excuses and have found ways to quell the soft voice.

GOD's voice is perhaps prompting you to GO. If you want to leave a legacy, you cannot stay put. You need to get moving; not as per your own will but in accordance with His voice.

When you GO; He straightens your path, paves the way, and provides the direction and as you follow His direction, you have taken the first step towards leaving a legacy.

My Reflections...

My Response...

My Actions...

PRINCIPLE 2

Envision a Future That Is Much Larger Than You

> **Genesis 12:1-3** 1 *Now the Lord said to Abram, "Get out of your country, From your family And from your father's house, To a land that I will show you.* 2 *I will make you a great nation; I will bless you And make your name great; And you shall be a blessing.* 3 *I will bless those who bless you, And I will curse him who curses you; And in you all the families of the earth shall be blessed."*

Envisioning a future that is distinctly different from your current reality is imperative for leaving a legacy.

When God said, "get out of your country, from your family to a land I will show you and further, I will make you a great nation, I will bless you and make your name great," and in the latter part of verse 3, "in you, all the families of the earth shall be blessed." That was a great vision for Abram to perhaps fathom but he envisioned what was said and he embarked on that journey. Envisioning a future that is distinctly different from your current reality is imperative for leaving a legacy.

This calls for some fundamental mind shifts. Outlined here below are four key areas to focus on:

a. Risk With The Calling Rather Than Languish In The Safety Of Your Comfort Net

You frequently find comfort in the familiar and decide that this is the best position to be in. You are unwilling to consider other possibilities or to look at the unfamiliar. According to Jeff Stafford in 'Complacency: A Leadership Tell', one of the five challenges to leadership effectiveness is a sense of complacency. When complacency grips you, it takes root, and you find yourself in a place of inaction or minimal action. You are called not for a comfortable life but for a controlled life – a Spirit-controlled life – where you perhaps are directed to the wilderness like Jesus, to be tested, or to chains and trials as Apostle Paul. But the willingness to take a risk with Him is much more effective than a life without risks.

It is interesting to note that the calling spells out the need to move out of different layers of comfort; go out of the country – cross boundaries of comfort, leave your family – that is perhaps the most familiar surroundings, where your guard is at its lowest and where you are most at ease, where you can be you without any mask. He also says, 'go to a land I will show you'; that is perhaps the heights of uncertainty, where you are required to embark on the journey without knowing the destination – that is taking a risk with Him. You trust the calling so much that you are willing to walk the way He paves for you without knowing where it leads. I remember when my daughter was three years old she used to love climbing. At one time, she was perched on a pedestal which was at a height of about nine feet, and did not know how to climb down. I reached out my hand and told her to jump and without hesitation she did. That is the level of dependence you need to have on His word.

If He is calling you to go yonder, move in line with the vision; don't hold back. Often as you risk with Him there is a temptation to think that everything will be hunky dory. That is not true; things will not all be cushions and roses; you will experience a fair share of thistles and thorns, which is what we find Abram experienced.

b. Risks Bring Returns

Abraham risked himself in response to the calling. The risk he undertook brought returns that he never would have access to had he stayed in the comfort of his home. Why do I say that?

> Genesis 12:7 *Then the LORD appeared to Abram and said, "To your descendants, I will give this land." And there he built an altar to the LORD, who had appeared to him.*

What blessings did Abram receive?

i. The Lord appeared. Isn't that wonderful? Often one goes on a yatra seeking god. One travels to the Holy land of Jerusalem, Haridwar, Kashi, Mecca, or Medina. Abram did none of that but the Lord appeared to him; that is what the calling does! He does far beyond what you can imagine!

ii. He did not merely appear but He said "To your descendants, I will give this land." Very often, you may strive to build a legacy, you may contrive to pull together a legacy that you want to leave behind. But this is an important truth I want you to remember – it is He who shapes your legacy as you are open to His leading you will find His hand orchestrating the varied aspects of your life and the universe shall appear to come together in one accord to your aid in spelling out your legacy for you.

c. Ensure You Schedule 'Me' Time In Your Diary

The latter part of verse 7 says, *"And there he built an altar to the Lord!"* And further, in verse 8 we find, *"He again built an altar unto the Lord."* If you want to leave a legacy, you need to find opportunities to have a 'me time' with Him and that will provide the necessary enablement to tide over the challenges that are likely to come your way. Do you have a personal altar? A family altar?

Any stalwart who has touched and influenced generations has consistently raised an altar and had a personal walk with Him regularly. According to reports, several students paid a visit to John Wesley's home, the man who founded the Methodist movement. Two marks on the floor were thought to mark the location where Wesley frequently knelt in prayer in one of the guestrooms. A student was absent when the tour was over and the group boarded the bus. When his professor followed in their footsteps, the missing student was discovered kneeling in the same position as John Wesley and fervently pleading with God, "O Lord, do it again! Do it once again, Lord!" Do you know the name of the student? It was Billy Graham. He left a legacy that affected more than 3.2 million people all over the world.

d. While The Vision Is Clear The Path To Realizing The Vision Is Often Beset With Challenges.

> Genesis 12:9-10 [9] *Abram kept moving, steadily making his way south, to the Negev.* [10] *Then a famine came to the land. Abram went down to Egypt to live; it was a hard famine.*

If you are to leave a legacy, you will need to expect and experience challenges. Abram experienced a famine. Your life circumstances are His emissaries to shape your legacy. Do not run away from those circumstances; instead, embrace them with open arms, for often the challenges you encounter unlock opportunities that you never thought possible. Several decades ago as Corporate Manager, managing the Training and Development function, working closely with the CEO, hobnobbing with senior management of a Tata organisation, and dining with the best in the executive dining room with access to multi-cuisine delicacies, I had a comfortable job, one that many would dream of. But when the opportunity to join a global consulting company, whose antecedents were not well known came up, I was seriously tempted to be comfortable in the known territory with all the comforts it offered, but in line with the nudging of the Spirit, I leapt in faith, and it opened out a range of possibilities, including visiting 32+ countries. Risk with Him.

You will possibly experience famines, failures, and frailties. When uncertainties of the unknown loom large, be assured that the Lord who has called you is faithful, and when you find yourself in sticky situations, He shall fight your battles. He shall pick up your cause. Why do I say that?

> Genesis 12:17 *But the Lord plagued Pharaoh and his house with great plagues because of Sarai, Abram's wife.*

He is not a stranger to the pain that you go through; if you are hurting and are in pain if you are fearful of the future and are anxious, this is His word for you: The future that He has in store for you is significantly greater than the fears that currently hold you back. Take Him at His word, He says, in

> Jeremiah 29:11 *"For I know the plans I have for you," declares the Lord, "plans to prosper you and not to harm you, plans to give you a hope and a future."*

As you experience those challenging situations, you possibly wonder if you should turn back and leave. When encountered with the famine, Abram possibly had a strong reason to go back. But the legacy he had to leave behind pulled him, the vision that he was aligned to propelled him forward, and the call he received got him to progress forward. He decided to move to Egypt in line with the direction of His call, and there again he was confronted with politics at the highest places, and his natural reaction was to pack up and leave as he had every reason to do so. But he stayed on. Remember that your current situation has no semblance to what He has promised, and it is when you stay on despite the challenges that you are in a position to craft your legacy.

It's often in the nothingness, emptiness, and pain that He does His most magnificent work! Remember, no matter what you are going through, He will see you through. "Abram, you followed me to the unknown and that is counted as faithfulness," says He. I am possibly nudging an Abram today - if you read this and there is a tug in your heart - do not quell that voice, for He is shaping a legacy for you and is with you co-creating that legacy.

My Reflections…

My Response…

My Actions…

PRINCIPLE 3

Choose Significance Over Success

Legacy builders and those who leave a legacy are those that choose significance over success. The way I define success is, it is more near-term and mid-term focused whereas significance is focused on a more long-term. While success is primarily self-centred, significance is others-centred. While success invariably focuses on self-advancement, significance focuses on collective advancement.

> *While success invariably focuses on self-advancement, significance focuses on collective advancement.*

So while you may be successful, you may not be significant; you cannot be significant without being successful, and thus, being significant is a step up over being successful. A key distinction is that one may be a very successful businessman but may not be viewed as significantly altering the lives of individuals; however, there are a few who are hugely successful and have gone on to become highly significant. The likes of JRD Tata, and Warren Buffet, among others, as businessmen were very successful but as philanthropists, they made a significant difference to the lives of others. So how do you choose significance over success?

a. Ensure A Line Of Sight Of Your Team And Your Area Of Operations:

> Genesis 13:5-7 [5] *Lot, who was travelling with Abram, was also rich in sheep and cattle and tents.* [6] *But the land couldn't support both of them; they had too many possessions. They couldn't both live there –* [7] *quarrels broke out between Abram's shepherds and Lot's shepherds. The Canaanites and Perizzites were also living on the land at the time.*

As you pursue significance, your operations will grow. Your influence will abound, your impact will increase, and soon the expanse of your work will grow multi-fold, and you are likely to be so embroiled in the expansions that you lose track of on-the-ground issues. There could be several simmering concerns that need your attention and need to be resolved early on. Develop a line of sight for potential cracks, growing differences, or on-the-ground issues that could result in severe damage to the relationship.

Keep your ears to the ground and pick up signals from your listening posts, your coworkers, and your interfaces; validate those reports and take corrective actions before it becomes too late and the differences become irreconcilable. Abram was sensitive to the growing differences on the ground. In your quest for significance and building a legacy, you need to be extremely sensitive to the movements on the ground. Often the weakest link is in the front line – keep a strong, steady line of sight on the front line.

b. Break Loose The Fetters That Bind You

> **Genesis 13:8-9** [8]*Abram said to Lot, "Let's not have fighting between us, between your shepherds and my shepherds. After all, we're family. Look around.* [9]*Isn't there plenty of land out there? Let's separate. If you go left, I'll go right; if you go right, I'll go left."*

> **Genesis 14:14-16** [14]*When Abram heard that his relative had been taken captive, he called out the 318 trained men born in his household and went in pursuit as far as Dan.* [15] *During the night Abram divided his men to attack them and he routed them, pursuing them as far as Hobah, North of Damascus.* [16]*He recovered all the goods and brought back his relative Lot and his possessions, together with the women and the other people.*

No matter how concrete the ties are, how compelling the bindings are, or how convenient the arrangement is, certain ties need to be snapped for your good and the good of your legacy. This is essentially what Abram did. There are those relationships, such as that of Abram and Lot that takes too much time, effort, and bandwidth with little or no value addition. Those ties suck your time, sap your energies, and saturate your mind. They offer little by way of reciprocity in terms of your growth, guidance, or glory. When you recognise such relationships it is best to snap those lest it grows into cancerous cells that eat into your legacy.

Be ruthless in dealing with such individuals and situations and do not let the bonding of love make compromises. I am not advocating you have nothing to do with such people in your life. But, as Abram did when Lot was in trouble, he reached out to Lot, destroyed the enemy, and saved Lot; you may possibly lend a helping hand to such. What I am saying is to be mindful of the fetters that bind you from achieving your vision, building your legacy, and leaving your legacy behind. It is those ties that need to be broken. There are certain ties where, I believe, there is a reason for you to strive tooth and nail to protect. For example, a relationship such as a marriage. Remember the Writ, "what God has put together, let man not put asunder." Thus, there is every reason for you to go multiple miles to ensure the relationship weathers the strife and discord and is thus best preserved. There are those ties that you need to nourish and nurture, and there are those ties that need to be negated and nullified. Choose wisely.

> **Genesis 13:14-17** [14]*The* L*ORD* said to Abram after Lot had
> parted from him, "Look around from where you are,
> to the *North and south, to the east and west.* [15]*All the*
> *land that you see I will give to you and your offspring*
> *forever.* [16]*I will make your offspring like the dust of*
> *the earth, so that if anyone could count the dust, then*
> *your offspring could be counted.* [17]*Go, walk through the*
> *length and breadth of the land, for I am giving it to*
> *you."*

Once the fetters are broken, it opens up new vistas of blessings, a new level of abundance, and a new horizon of possibilities that you never thought possible. When the chord between Abram and Lot was snapped, it opened out a new world of blessings for Abram. All that Abram saw was his! That is the legacy that opens up for you when you break loose of the fetters that bind you and pulls you down!

c. See The Unseen Opportunities Of The Future Rather Than The Obvious Outlook Of The Present

A distinct feature of those choosing significance over success is their capability to see what others don't ever see. They are neither beguiled by the allures of the present-day environment nor bewitched by the attractions of the here and the now. They see the potential in the barrenness and the power beneath the blandness with GOD being the primary mover. Abram's classical statement is a reflection of this strong conviction – he says to Lot, "If you take the left, I will go the right, if you take the right, I will take the left." What a sense of confidence in the calling he had.

Legacy builders develop a strong understanding of what they can do with little or nothing + the divine. This in turn guides their thinking and directs their actions. When you develop perspective and begin to see as He sees rather than as man sees it, you are taking definite steps towards building your legacy. Remember the Biblical injunction:

> I Samuel 16:7 *Man looks at the outward appearance but the Lord looks at the heart.*

It calls for tremendous discipline for you to steer away from the external pulls and focus on the internal ones. When you do that, He who sees the inside of you rewards you so bountifully since you surmised that with God on your side you are stronger, smarter, and savvier than the seemingly better options. When you seek significance the outcomes are significantly more impactful than being successful. Why? You see the legacy being shaped not by human hands, but by the divine.

> **Genesis 13:16-17** [16]*And I will make your descendants as the dust of the earth; so that if a man could number the dust of the earth, then your descendants also could be numbered.* [17]*Arise, walk in the land through its length and its width, for I give it to you."*

There is a definitiveness about this future – the land promised to the descendants is given! What a privilege it is to see unseen opportunities. May you be gifted to choose significance over success and thus positively impact the legacy you leave behind.

My Reflections...

My Response...

My Actions...

PRINCIPLE 4

Play for the Long Term and Shun the Short-Term Fixes

The legacy builders ensure they are laser-focused on the longer term. No matter how compelling the short-term fixes are, they stay clear of the short-term compromises. They operate on a different work ethic that prioritizes the longer term over the shorter term. They subscribe to a work ethos that consistently keeps the longer term as the reference point. All strategic actions are viewed through the lens of the long term. Highlighted below are three key lessons from the life of Abram that reiterates this longer-term focus.

a. Value People More Than Goods

> **Genesis 14:22-23** 22 *"But Abram said to the king of Sodom, "With raised hand I have sworn an oath to the LORD, God Most High, Creator of heaven and earth,* 23th*at I will accept nothing belonging to you, not even a thread or the strap of a sandal so that you will never be able to say, 'I made Abram rich'."*

We get a peek into the mindset of Abram. Wealth was being offered to him by the king of Sodom and all Abram needed to do was to accede to his request and leave behind the people to take the wealth. Abram's view is defining. He saw the value of

They value the souls more than the stocks, people more than the products, workers more than the work, artisans more than the artefacts, and mankind more than the merchandise.

people to be much higher than wealth and thus did not trade people. He did not want to trade souls for the soup. In a world where goods are treasured and people trampled upon, where wealth is accumulated and women and men are alienated, legacy builders operate with a reverse mindset. They value the souls more than the stocks, people more than the products, workers more than the work, artisans more than the artefacts, and mankind more than the merchandise. What a sad reversal of priorities we see today.

During one of my client engagements, the CEO of a top-notch technology company said, "Every morning we wait with bated breath to see if our most precious resources will walk back into our corridors." This was from the CEO of a high-tech global company. People are far more valuable than possessions. If you want to be a legacy builder, you must have this deeply embedded in your psyche. Often, we have leaders who pay lip service to the importance they ascribe to people. You, like many, may say the right things concerning treasuring people – but in reality, when making crucial decisions, do people come out as your top priority? If not, you perhaps need to do some rethinking.

b. Endeavour To Rewrite The Norms

Many are happy to fall in sync, toe the line, and not ruffle feathers even when it is the right thing to do. Abram was different. He did not accept the allure of easy money, instead presented an interesting perspective in verse 23; Abram did not want to attribute his riches to a man and he said, "I will not take anything that is yours, lest you should say, I have made Abram rich." Legacy builders do not follow the script. They rewrite the script; what an amazing perspective! This was a guiding verse in my life as I moved to the city from a small town, and despite the possibility of staying with a close blood relative who graciously offered their place for me to reside, I desisted, as whatever I become in life I was keen should be attributed to GOD and not to any man.

In December 2021, Germany bid farewell to Angela Merkel, the chancellor of Germany. With six minutes of applause on the streets and roads, by-lanes and by-ways, balconies and windows, the whole country applauded the spectacular leadership of this exemplary statesperson for 18 years. During this period of leadership not a single transgression was recorded against her, not any of her relatives were assigned to government offices, and she was un-tempted by the glamour of the world and did not buy properties or luxury cars or private planes. She was questioned during a press conference: "We see you wearing the same suit, don't you have any other?" She retorted, "I am a government employee and not a model." When specifically questioned at another news conference, she admitted that she and her husband did all the housework and had no servants. What a fantastic life where the welfare of others comes before one's own, where the public good comes before individual wealth. Legacy builders are made like that. You do not follow the pattern of the world, but re-scribe the pattern and stick to those high standards denying plausible pleasures of this world as you are concerned about making or shaping a different world!

c. Believe In The Impossible And Exercise Mountain-Moving Faith

> Genesis 15:5-6 5 *Then he took him outside and said, "Look at the sky. Count the stars. Can you do it? Count your descendants!* 6 *You're going to have a big family, Abram!" And he believed!*

> *Legacy builders are wired to dream the implausible, dare the improbable, and do the impossible. When everyone says it is not doable, legacy builders exercise their faith and through the eyes of faith see that which others fail to see.*

Legacy builders are wired to dream the implausible, dare the improbable, and do the impossible. When everyone says it is not doable, legacy builders exercise their faith and through the eyes of faith see that which others fail to see. I would like you to picturise this. God brings the old man Abram, whose wife Sarai was barren, out in the open and said, *"Look at the heavens and count the stars if you can – so shall your descendants be,"* verse 6 says, and Abram believed. There are three key lessons you may pick up.

i. Legacy builders believe in a future that is much larger than themselves.

ii. Legacy builders look beyond their immediate circumstances, situations, or problems onto a future state that is significantly higher than their current reality.

iii. Legacy builders subscribe to a higher code beyond themselves.

Amid the impossible, legacy builders see possibilities. In the midst of the unimaginable, legacy builders create feasibilities. Several years ago, when the organisation I was working for launched a product, there was scepticism rampant about making a sale. I recognised the power of the product and put together a presentation with all the USPs, distinct advantages, technical specs, and the difference it can make to the client. No one in the team believed we could make the sale including my colleague, the Sales Director. But I wanted to prove that it was possible to make the sale. I persevered with the client, made multiple calls, engaged in numerous closed-door meetings, and presentations, and closed a sale to the tune of 10 million, which was the highest-ever sale of a single product. JK Rowling's first Harry Potter book allegedly received 12 rejections before being accepted and released. The renowned basketball player Michael Jordan lost hundreds of games and missed thousands of shots over his career, but he said, "I have failed again, and over and over again, which is why I succeed." Believe in the impossible and the impossible will become possible.

My Reflections…

My Response…

My Actions…

PRINCIPLE 5

Pivot Into a Significantly Larger Dimension of Your Life

For you to pivot effectively, you are required to sharpen your focus on the vision of the desired state and pursue your vision relentlessly. To pivot your life, it is good practice to start with a diagnosis of where you are on the 'Life-Pivot Framework' which includes the crucial parameters of life and these could be:

- Spiritual wellbeing
- Physical wellbeing
- Social wellbeing
- Career wellbeing
- Financial wellbeing
- Growth wellbeing

You may add any other parameter that you consider important to this list. The idea is to plot yourself on a 7-point scale on where you are on each of these parameters today where 1 is "Needs significant improvement" and 7 is "Zenith". Draw a scale horizontally with numbers 1 to 7 captured on top and vertically on the left of the page write down the parameters you identified. The task is to reflect on how satisfied you are currently with each of the parameters and mark it with a cross symbol in that continuum. This is your satisfaction index.

Now review the areas that are marked as 3, 4, or 5. These are the areas that you need to consider afresh. These are typically the mediocre areas that you settle in. The point is you cannot both be satisfied and unsatisfied and the truth is that there are areas that either work or do not work, so recalibrate those areas and then focus on the areas that are marked 1, 2, and 6, 7. Shade the 1 and 2 in yellow and the areas assessed as 6 and 7 in green. The areas that are marked as 1 and 2 are those that you need to pivot. When you pivot those areas you experience a breakthrough in your life. I would like to highlight three areas that should motivate you to pivot.

a. The Pull Of The Promised Land

> Genesis 17:5-6,8 [5] *"No longer shall your name be called Abram, but your name shall be Abraham; for I have made you a father of many nations.* [6]*I will make you exceedingly fruitful, and I will make nations of you, and kings shall come from you."*
>
> [8] *"Also I give to you and your descendants after you the land in which you are a stranger, all the land of Canaan, as an everlasting possession."*

The promise is for a geometric expansion of gigantic proportions far beyond what you can fathom. Which is what happened with Abram. He was promised that he shall be called Abraham, the father of many nations. Further, he was given a glimpse of the promised land. If you want to leave a legacy keep a line of sight on the promised land; the future that you would like to leave behind for generations behind you should aid you to pivot the areas that call for a tweak.

How do you keep the flame of the promised land alive? I recommend a threefold formula:

i. Keep your eyes fixed on the land of milk and honey – the promised land, and do not allow distractions to detract you.

ii. Engage in value-adding activities that can provide you leverage when you enter the promised land, e.g., reading about leadership, getting on top of new technology, etc.

iii. Resist the attractions of the 'here and the now' in view of the promised land, or in other words, defer your present pleasures in pursuit of future possibilities.

A good friend of mine from a Zamindari family, a handsome dude invariably had many girls and women courting him. There was an occasion when a woman threw herself at him, and he desisted, as he had a line of sight of the promised land and did not want to give in to the fleeting pleasures of the flesh and sear his conscience with guilt. His legacy will script a story that is distinctly different from the run-of-the-mill men who do not desist from the pleasures of the flesh and destroy their lives in the bargain; for the addiction induced by the other man/woman has the potential to deviate you from the promised land.

You are familiar with Mohammed Ali, the boxing world champion. During one of the interviews, Phil Donahue asked him a question, "What is the central part of your training? Is it running? Is it training? What is it?" And Ali's answer shocked the entire audience and beyond. "It's dodging the night clubs and the parties and the girls. Being in bed by yourself at 9:00 p.m. If you can get by that you will make it." He continued, "…Hitting the bags and jogging and vitamins don't. Dodging ladies is the main thing, especially when you are pretty like me."

Let the pull of the promised land be so compelling that the pushes of the pleasures are of no attraction in comparison.

b. The Force Of Faith

Faith makes the impossible possible, it creates possibilities beyond imagination and it brings in a future that never existed and births a reality that was never real.

Faith is a conviction to take Him at His word and follow the vision no matter what. Faith is a commitment to see beyond the obstacles onto the promise. Faith is the courage to move forward when circumstances tell you otherwise. For you to pivot the vision, it calls for a supernatural faith that can hardly be described but is consistently exercised, which elevates you from an ordinary Jack or plain Jane to an extraordinary Raja (king) or super Raja! That is the power of faith. That is what Abram did; unleash faith far beyond his physical limitations, mental blocks and environmental constraints. Faith makes the impossible possible, it creates possibilities beyond imagination and it brings in a future that never existed and births a reality that was never real. How do you exercise such a supernatural faith?

i. Have a crystal clear vision of the future.

ii. See not the enormity of the vision but fix your eyes on Him who can help you achieve that vision.

iii. Trust Him implicitly – a childlike faith to make what is impossible possible. Hebrews 11 is a treatise to faith that I would encourage you to read in-depth.

c. The Engineering Of Eternity

Legacy builders are constantly thinking about living beyond themselves; they are concerned about how they will be remembered after they pass on from this earth into eternity. Two key elements are important to bear in mind:

i. Legacy builders focus not merely on the things of the earth from a "what do I want to be remembered as" mindset, but their focus is on the things of eternal value – "what values am I nurturing from an afterlife standpoint?"

ii. Abraham was not merely thinking of his lifetime; in fact, he physically saw only his son and his grandson, but with the eyes of faith he saw the future generations and the rich legacy he was leaving behind for multiple generations to come. Thus shifting the focus from the immediate to eternity has a telling effect.

Perhaps, it is useful for you to ask yourself: what legacy do you want to leave behind for the generations to come from a physical standpoint and more importantly from a spiritual perspective?

My Reflections…

My Response…

My Actions…

PRINCIPLE 6

Beware of the Snares That Can Take Away the Legacy

Every farmer is concerned about the weeds, every shepherd is concerned about the black sheep, every software developer is concerned about the bugs, every leader is concerned about the follower gone astray, and every legacy builder should be concerned about the snares that can derail the legacy that (s)he meticulously builds. Within the scriptures, there is a reference to little foxes that ruin the vineyard:

> Song of Songs 2:15 *"Catch for us the foxes, the little foxes that ruin the vineyards, our vineyards that are in bloom"*

These little foxes are little follies that destroy the vine and when the vineyards are unattended:

a. Watch Out, For Haste Makes Waste

> Genesis 16:1-4 [1] *Now Sarai, Abram's wife, had borne him no children. And she had an Egyptian maidservant whose name was Hagar.* [2] *So Sarai said to Abram, "See now, the LORD has restrained me from bearing children. Please, go in to my maid; perhaps I shall obtain children by her."* [3] *And Abram heeded the voice of Sarai. Then Sarai, Abram's wife, took Hagar her maid, the Egyptian,*

and gave her to her husband Abram to be his wife after Abram had dwelt ten years in the land of Canaan. So he went in to Hagar, and she conceived.

Sarai, Abram's wife was in a hurry to get a son and so hastened Abram to take Hagar to have a son through her. Abram fell in line – like most men. Haste is a destructive force; it destroys fully. Haste is the reason for many falls, several mistakes, numerous oversights, and innumerable accidents. Haste is cutting corners to meet the objectives but in the process runs the risk of missing the objectives. As part of the Tata organisation in the early days of my service, we were entrusted with putting an application to the JRDQV Awards, the prestigious Tata Business Excellence Awards mirrored after the Malcolm Baldridge Quality criteria. As part of the core team working on putting up the application, we were racing against time and worked non-stop for 52 hours. In a bid to meet the timeline, a core team member wrote out a response to one of the criteria on the wrong premise which had to be rewritten, and that put enormous pressure on the entire core team.

More recently, you may have heard of the CEO of Better.com the company touted to be a Fintech organisation that called a group of 900 or so employees on a call and fired them. His intention was perhaps to prune the organisation and make it profitable, but the way he did it by insensitively firing people on a call went viral and generated such a massive volley of anti-sentiment that he was sent out on forced leave. The learning is to be deliberate rather than hasty, take time to do some thinking before acting, and consider consequences fully before jumping in and doing only to repent at leisure.

Wait for His timing no matter how lonely it gets, no matter how attractive the counsels appear or how compelling the arguments may seem.

Abram and Sarai were in a hurry and were unwilling to wait for the right time. The right time designated was 14 years later, but Ishmael was born 14 years earlier than the promised son, Isaac. When you short-circuit His plans and allow your plans to supersede His plans, you birth an Ishmael. Wait for His timing no matter how lonely it gets, no matter how attractive the counsels appear or how compelling the arguments may seem. Sarai's counsel seemingly appeared to be the right course of action. There could be counsels that you hear that your ears itch to hear and you think that He has spoken, but the truth is you have forgotten His promises and have resorted to dubious means to achieve what He said He would do.

What is it that He has promised you and you have endeavoured to expedite before the due time? He does everything in due time. Abraham, don't try to push Him! Wait patiently for things to fall into place and they will. In a world where speed is everything, this is counterintuitive. However, remember that haste makes waste but thoughtfulness always results in thoroughness which in turn leads to triumph.

b. Watch Out For Allowing Subjective Emotions To Precede Objective Imperatives

One of the biggest snares that come between you and the legacy you endeavor to leave behind is misreading circumstances and taking the counterfeit to be genuine. Placing your bets on the wrong guy is the death knell to your legacy. You are often moved by emotions and allow them to colour your vision, and your objectivity is compromised. Once you let subjectivity take the upper hand, your decisions are coloured and the consequences are colossal. One of our clients, a multi-business conglomerate, went ahead with their subjective assessment for a succession much against the objective assessment shared by us and promoted a highly driven business individual only to find he lacked significant people skills and had to recant their decision in a matter of two years.

> Genesis 17:17-18 [17]*Then Abraham fell on his face and laughed, and said in his heart, "Shall a child be born to a man who is one hundred years old?* [18]*And shall Sarah, who is ninety years old, bear a child?" And Abraham said to God, "Oh, that Ishmael might live before You!"*

Here you find Abraham making a plausible request, *"Oh that Ishmael might live before you!"* And He being the gracious Person He is, who accedes to the requests of His people, granted the request of Abraham, and to this day the descendants of Ishmael are a constant thorn to the nation of Israel. When you shift your focus away from the purpose you are called to achieve, the legacy you are to leave behind, and give in to the pleasures of your sentiments and subjective interpretations, there is high certainty that you will put your legacy at risk.

c. Watch Out For Lapses In Integrity

Integrity is an essential ingredient to leave a lasting legacy. When compromises are made to integrity, it runs the risk of exposing you to undue stress, eating into your credibility and sense of worth. Small lapses in integrity can cost you dearly and significantly. If you want to leave a lasting legacy, there is enormous sense in determining early on where you will not make compromises; that decision will go a long way in ensuring a life without lapses in integrity.

When I was young, a friend and I travelled by train. When we reached home, I gloated to my dad that I did not buy a ticket and the ticket checker did not catch me. My dad got my friend and me to cycle back to the railway station which was at a distance of three to four kms, buy a ticket, and tear up the ticket. The learning was clear. If you use a service, you have to pay for it regardless of whether you are watched or not. You are watched by the invisible eyes of the Lord above. That was a lesson for life.

> **Genesis 12:11-13** 11*And it came to pass, when he was close to entering Egypt, that he said to Sarai his wife, "Indeed I know that you are* a woman of beautiful countenance.
> 12 *Therefore it will happen, when the Egyptians see you, that they will say, 'This is* his wife'; and they will kill me, but they will let you live. 13*Please say you are* my sister, that it may be well with me for your sake, and that I may live because of you."

Abram colludes with his wife and gets her to speak lies to the Egyptian king; the intent was to protect himself – which is a survival instinct; no problem with the survival instinct; however, the ramifications of that could have devoured his wife, decimated his peace of mind and destroyed his legacy. So how do you ensure you don't get ensnared? In the words of Andre De Shields, you do three things: 1. Surround yourself with people whose eyes light up when they see you coming. 2. Slowly is the fastest way to where you want to be. 3. The top of one mountain is the bottom of the next, so keep climbing!

My Reflections…

My Response…

My Actions…

PRINCIPLE 7

Periods of Testing Determines Your Mettle; Expect Testing Times

If you are to leave a legacy, you can rest assured that you will have to go through periods of intense testing; for some, it could be walking through fire, for others, it could be being thrown in the lion's den and yet for others it could be braving the stormy seas. Whatever the testing that you are required to go through – you will be tested for sure – for testing has a powerful quality of calling out who you are. You know that when carbon goes through significant pressure over long periods of time, it either crystallises into diamond or dissipates into coal. It is the testing of pressure that reveals the diamonds. Let us look at the life of Abraham and see how this testing paved the way for him to leave a legacy. Let me highlight three crucial elements that you need to bear in mind as you go through those periods of testing and endeavour to build a legacy.

> **Genesis 22:2-3** 2 *Then He said, "Take now your son, your only son Isaac, whom you love, and go to the land of Moriah, and offer him there as a burnt offering on one of the mountains of which I shall tell you."* 3 *So Abraham rose*

> *early in the morning and saddled his donkey, and took two of his young men with him, and Isaac his son; and he split the wood for the burnt offering, and arose and went to the place of which God had told him.*

a. Win Those Battles And The War Is Yours!

> *You cannot win the war if you have lost the battles, but you will do well to keep the line of sight on the war when fighting your battles.*

Following Him was easy for Abram. When God said, "Go" he did just that! This made it easy for him to follow God when He said, "sacrifice your son." Taking Him at His word in everyday actions is a pre-requisite for taking Him at His word for crucial or orbit-shifting decisions. Remember the principle; if you are faithful in the little things, you will be entrusted with bigger things. You cannot win the war if you have lost the battles, but you will do well to keep the line of sight on the war when fighting your battles.

For you to leave a legacy impacting millions, you need to be willing to follow the dictates of the Writ as is. Why? The biggest fall of man/woman is owing to the biggest lapse of not following the biggest dictate in the garden of Eden at the beginning of the saga of life. The deceptive serpent in the garden of Eden at the beginning of life on Earth is alive and active today at the end of times, doing his best to draw you away from following the Writ. The decision is yours, whose voice you amplify and yield to.

You may wonder what is the connection between following His dictates and the legacy you leave behind. The first Adam did not follow the statute and the legacy he left behind is that of sin, strife, and slavery. On the contrary, the second Adam followed the heart of God and left behind a legacy that you can enjoy today – of salvation, sanctification, and satisfaction. The point is when you follow His word in the little things, it reinforces trust and you can take Him at His word on larger things. Within the corporate world when you are required to make a pitch for a critical multi-million dollar project who would you front-end that presentation? It is someone who has proved himself or herself in the past, right? That same principle works here; when you have proven yourself in following His dictates in small things, He gains confidence in you and entrusts you with big things. Remember the Biblical injunction, in Luke 16:10 – *"Whoever is faithful in very little will also be faithful with much."*

b. When He Leads, He Provides!

> Genesis 22: 6-8 6 *So Abraham took the wood of the burnt offering and laid it on Isaac his son; he took the fire in his hand, and a knife, and the two of them went together.* 7 *But Isaac spoke to Abraham his father and said, "My father!" And he said, "Here I am, my son." Then he said, "Look, the fire and the wood, but where is the lamb for a burnt offering?"* 8 *And Abraham said, "My son, God will provide for Himself the lamb for a burnt offering." So the two of them went together.*

> Genesis 22: 13 *Then Abraham lifted his eyes and looked, and there behind him was a ram caught in a thicket by its horns. So Abraham went and took the ram, and offered it up for a burnt offering instead of his son.*

Surrendering to His leading is equable to trusting Him for His provision. Consider Abraham's confidence. In response to the innocent question of his beloved son, "Where is the lamb for the offering?" Abraham responds, "The Lord will provide." This is not a glib answer to shut his son off, but a genuine understanding. And the Lord did provide a ram for the offering!

Following His leading step by step ensures His will is not thwarted even when the situation is grim. There can be times when you find yourself in a place where you don't know where the funds, support, or numbers would come from, but as you follow His leading, He provides and never fails.

My parents' family income dropped significantly to Rs. 500/- in the early 1980s when they transitioned into full-time mission work, giving up their lucrative positions as a doctor with a thriving private practice and as a headmistress. We downsized from an eight-room bungalow to a one-room kitchen when I was a missionary kid. There were certain days when all we had was rasam, a hot South Indian soup, and rice, God was faithful and never allowed us to go without food. My father had the means to provide for us comfortably if he had so wished, but he chose to live modestly and within the resources that were allotted, and the Lord provided for our needs.

We learned so much during those times – going from luxury to hardship, and it has served us well now. It has bolstered our faith, enhanced our trust in God, and allowed us to rely on Him in all circumstances. I have witnessed the wonderful ways in which His provision has met our needs! When you follow His leading, He takes care of your needs and plans the provision in creative ways that defy comprehension.

c. The Measure Of Faith You Exercise Determines The Measure Of Returns You Derive

Do you know what faith is? Faith is taking God at His word and doing what He says, even if it makes no sense to you. Implicit childlike faith which says God has said it, I have done it, and that is all there is to it. Abraham's faith took him to the brink of sacrificing his son without a moment's hesitation. That faith brings returns far beyond what you can fathom. Abraham's act of faith had fashioned generations behind him who are known for their intelligence, industry, and innovation. That kind of faith gives you explicit returns.

My uncle had given me a priceless gold band and I felt a soft voice whispering into my ears to donate it to a missional need that came up. I wondered: is this God speaking to me, or are my emotions getting the better of me? I gave the ring away without hesitation once I was convinced that it was God prodding me. You know what? God honoured that faith and several years later the Lord blessed us with gold multiple times over the worth of the gold that I had invested into the needy. The measure of faith you exercise is the measure of returns you derive.

My Reflections…

My Response…

My Actions…

PRINCIPLE 8

Legacy Has a Compounding Effect Beyond Your Lifetime

The amazing fact about legacy is that it invariably compounds multi-fold beyond your lifetime. Your faithfulness in nourishing the legacy will continue to bloom and bring significant enhancement beyond time here on earth. For example, in Genesis 26, Isaac the son of Abraham lives out the legacy left behind by his father. I would like to highlight three key lessons from this passage for your consideration.

a. Your Faith Walk Ushers In A Hundredfold Advantage To The Next Generation

> Genesis 26:2,12 2 *Then the Lord appeared to him and said: "Do not go down to Egypt; live in the land of which I shall tell you."*
>
> 12 *Then Isaac sowed in that land, and reaped in the same year a hundredfold; and the Lord blessed him.*

Your faith walk creates opportunities for your children to walk in faith. If you are a parent and have children today who appear to be lost, given to addictions or given to earthly pursuits with no reference to the eternal context - this is a word for you. The God of Abraham initiates a relationship with Isaac just as He initiated a relationship with Abraham. You find the blessings enjoyed by Isaac because of the covenant established with his father. Here below, I have captured the text from Genesis 26 and the ensuing blessing alongside:

Verse	Text	Blessing
2	"Do not go down to Egypt; live in the land of which I shall tell you"	Prescription
3	"Dwell in this land…"	Provision
	"…and I will be with you and bless you…"	Providence
	"…for to you and your descendants, I give all these lands…"	Promise
	"…and I will perform the oath which I swore to Abraham your father"	Patronage
4	"And I will make your descendants multiply as the stars of heaven…"	Progeny
	"…I will give to your descendants all these lands"	Pledge
	"…and in your seed, all the nations of the earth shall be blessed"	Purpose
5	Why does He do this? "Because Abraham obeyed My voice and kept My charge, My commandments, My statutes, and My laws"	Prudence

Abraham's prudence resulted in multi-fold blessings for Isaac and his descendants. If you desire your children to be blessed, the mantra is to walk in faith and follow Him. And further, do you know the impact of all these blessings on the life of your children? Isaac sowed in that land and reaped a hundredfold in the same year, and the Lord blessed him. Hallelujah! Isaac sowed and God gave a 100-fold increase in the crop in the same year; that is productivity! That is the power of legacy. I encourage you to hold on to this promise for your children and your children's children. This is God's doing and no man can stop it!

b. Your Advancement Will Tickle The Eyes Of The Enemy And Generate Envy And Fear!

> Genesis 26:14 *for he had possessions of flocks and possessions of herds and a great number of servants. So the Philistines envied him.*

Your children's prominence will draw the attention of the political and the powerful. They will burn with envy at the prosperity and progress made by your children; "they were envious of Isaac," the account says. Further, a section will not want you and will endeavour to drive you out of its circles. Fear of your prowess and progress will result in rejection. Are you being rejected by certain circles? Let me assure you that this is part of the legacy building. If you are not rejected by certain circles then something is not right with you. Remember, Jesus was rejected by the Pharisees, He was rejected by His people, riled by the Roman soldiers, and wrangled by the powers of the day. But He emerged victorious and so shall you.

Others' envy shall surface in the roadblocks they create on your way, the dissensions that arise when they engage with you, and the discord that emerges in the course of normal conversations.

These are sure signs that you are doing something right, that you are striking the right chord. Do not get vexed; instead, note that you have made the right moves that have irked certain quarters, and that in turn deepens the opportunity to establish your legacy!

c. Resistance In The Workplace Is A Sure Sign Of Favour In Your Life

> **Genesis 26:18-22** [18]*And Isaac dug again the wells of water*
> *which they had dug in the days of Abraham his father,*
> *for the Philistines had stopped them up after the death*
> *of Abraham. He called them by the names which his*
> *father had called them.* [19]*Also Isaac's servants dug in the*
> *valley, and found a well of running water there.* [20]*But*
> *the herdsmen of Gerar quarrelled with Isaac's herdsmen,*
> *saying, "The water is ours." So he called the name of the*
> *well Esek because they quarrelled with him.* [21]*Then they*
> *dug another well, and they quarrelled over that one also.*
> *So he called its name Sitnah.* [22]*And he moved from there*
> *and dug another well, and they did not quarrel over it.*
> *So he called its name Rehoboth, because he said, "For*
> *now the LORD has made room for us, and we shall be*
> *fruitful in the land."*

The Philistines usurped the wells of Isaac's father, Abraham. There will be times when what is legitimately yours will be denied you. It rightfully belongs to you, and you have every right to take ownership of those wells but the Philistines staked claim to what was Isaac's. Consider Isaac's response. He did not react, he did not fight, he did not use muscle power, and he did not command his large array of servants who were at his call to obliterate them. Instead, he just moved away. He was an embodiment of meekness. It was as though he was following the footsteps of his father Abraham who said to Lot, "If you go North, I will go South." Here, Isaac merely moved away from the Philistines without argument. This was not a one-off occurrence. On multiple occasions, using the wells of his father Abraham was met with significant and consistent resistance. Isaac's response was equally consistent. What is the learning?

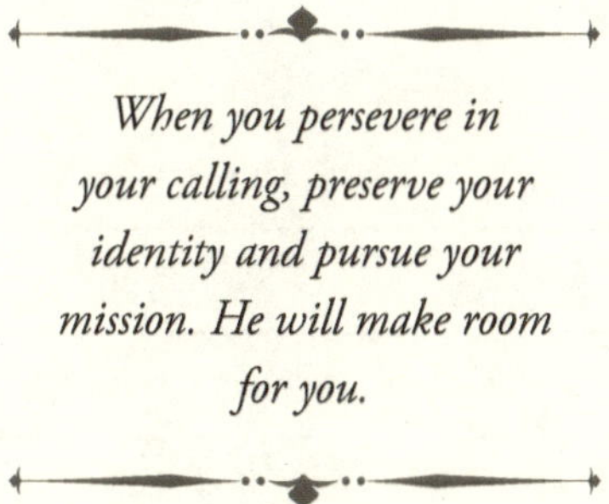

Don't blow up issues that are beneath you. Don't get drawn into squabbles that are not in line with the legacy that you need to nurture. Further, in the face of resistance don't react, don't give up but continue doing what you are required to do. When you persevere in your calling, preserve your identity and pursue your mission. He will make room for you – REHOBOTH. Isn't that wonderful? So don't strive where you should not, but surrender into His hands and He shall make a way where there seems no way. If you have resigned yourself because of your work situation, this is a word for you – *Rehoboth.* He is making a way for you, take hold of it, for that is the legacy that has been set for you which you will leave for your children.

My Reflections…

My Response…

My Actions…

– II –

Moses, the Meek and Mighty Leader

I would like to transition from the life of Abraham to the life of Moses, another one of the ancient leaders whose life was influential and impactful. One of the most significant figures in ancient global history, he lived around 1400 BC.

Moses was born to a Hebrew slave, and he grew up in the Egyptian king's court as a Prince of Egypt. When he recognised the rich heritage he had, he broke the convention and embarked on a journey that took him far away from the coveted throne of Egypt but won him the respect of and paved the way for the liberation of millions of Israelites, thus leaving a legacy behind for millenniums to cherish.

Often, a glamourous life with its trappings of unbridled power, opulent affluence, and uncurbed access is sought after, but a conscious call to take a departure from such a lifestyle and embrace a life of penury, abstinence, and simplicity is not a preferred path. But legacy builders often do just as Moses did. It is worthwhile to continue the legacy journey and glean insights from the life of Moses. Outlined below are four principles gleaned from his life that may be deemed to be common among legacy builders.

PRINCIPLE 9

Find Pressing Problems of Your People and Endeavour to Solve Them

Actions born out of burden may not always be right – act nevertheless: Inaction is the malady of most people. To act is to exercise mind and body and be intentional with action which arises out of volition. There is merit in action rather than inaction. Don't get me wrong. I am not advocating wrong actions what I am saying is to act rather than sit tight without acting in response to a need in your environment. For our learning, we shall consider three lessons from the life of Moses:

a. Be Moved By The Burden Of The Suffering Of Others

Identifying the need and endeavouring to address that need is the hallmark of a legacy builder. The much-acclaimed Shark Tank TV series which has Business Moghuls funding business ideas has one salient feature. Of all the business funding made, a significant percentage of funding was given to those who along with a brilliant business potential also had a unique need that was being met.

When you are so moved by and burdened with the issues on the ground, when you are so sensitive to pick up the on-the-ground realities and needs, when you have your eyes and ears tuned in to catch the needs that are obvious and often not so obvious, and you are convinced that you need to do something about it, you begin to spell the start of a revolution of such mammoth proportions – far beyond your wildest dreams.

History is replete with examples of men and women who identified a need and invested their lives in pursuit of addressing that need which turned the course of history. Abraham Lincoln identified a need to abolish slavery, Mahatma Gandhi was cognizant of the need for freedom, Martin Luther King Jr recognised the need for equal civil rights, and Nelson Mandela picked up the growing racial discrimination. The burden grew in their hearts and the burden was the springboard of significant change.

> Exodus 2:11 *Now it came to pass in those days, when Moses was grown, that he went out to his brethren and looked at their burdens. And he saw an Egyptian beating a Hebrew, one of his brethren.*

When Moses was grown, he went out to his brethren and looked at their burdens. The Writ says, *"And he saw an Egyptian beating a Hebrew, one of his brethren."*

What is your burden? Are you cognisant of the needs around you? Are you disturbed by the growing problems in your context? Do you see your brethren mistreated, communities gripped by poverty, and tribes languishing in abject deprivation of education, healthcare or sanitation? Have you taken the time and effort to understand their needs? If you have not, perhaps today is the day to start.

b. The Burden Should Lead To Action

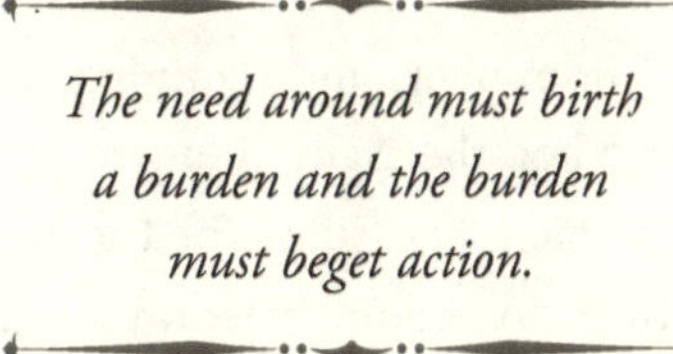

The need around must birth a burden and the burden must beget action.

When you are burdened and restless by the need around you and that need grows into a significant storm in your mind and takes your sleep away, it will prompt you to act. The acid test of a burden that it is alive and kicking, is action. Remember James 2:14, *"faith without action is dead,"* and I would dare say burden without commensurate action is doubly dead. The need around must birth a burden and the burden must beget action. Take any movement in the world, – the Quit India movement led by M.K. Gandhi or the civil rights movement led by Martin Luther King Jr, or the anti-apartheid movement led by Nelson Mandela – they were actions emerging from burdens culminating from the needs they sensed in their contexts.

You get a glimpse of Moses' action, here below:

> Exodus 2:12 *So he looked this way and that way, and when he saw no one, he killed the Egyptian and hid him in the sand.*

You cannot condone this action. However, the critical point to note is that the burden birthed an action. That sense of burden when it grips you invariably leads to something significant – something out of the ordinary, something earth-shattering. What actions has your burden birthed?

c. Inaction Is Worse Than Incorrect Action – Act Now

Moses's action when he was confronted by the injustice meted out to his people was reactive, imminent, and damning. In hindsight, we know that it was not the right thing to do. Perhaps Moses was one of those men who subscribed to the ethic – some action is better than no action. Inaction is the greatest malaise that has hit most; often the action may be wrong, but act. Often, the information may be incomplete but use the existing information and act. Ordinarily, there may be gaps in understanding all the facets of the problem, but act with whatever understanding you have. Organizations that have made significant strides in market capitalization and brand recall, consistently bring out cutting-edge products that are functional, of high quality, and on time, and do not wait for turning in the perfect versions. They operate on the premise that versions 2, 3, and 4 will be better with improvements to the existing product.

Moses acted – legacy builders act; do you act in response to the burden or do you merely pay lip service; let your lip service become less of lip service and more of lip-less service and birth actions that can have significant outcomes.

My Reflections...

My Response...

My Actions...

PRINCIPLE 10

Passion Drives Purpose

Passion is what makes purpose come alive. As a consultant having worked with some of the best CEOs and CXOs in several marquee organizations, if I were to be asked what differentiates the truly successful leaders from the mediocre ones without hesitation, I would say 'passion'. Yes, vision is important, strategy is critical, and operations are imperative. But passion overrides them all; for it is the passion that gets you to go back repeatedly through the failures, through the tough times and make that purpose come alive. I would like to highlight three key lessons on passion from the life of Moses that are critical from a legacy-builder standpoint:

a. Passion Is Not A One-Time Activity; It Is A Timeless Endeavour

I have seen committed high performing individuals who make a song and dance about TGIF; Thank God It's Friday. I don't have anything against those who celebrate Friday and the oncoming weekend, but I have a serious concern about people paying lip service to what they term as passion – it is not something to flirt with and dump; it is an investment of a lifetime into what you are passionate about. Whatever the area of your passion, are you willing to give it continued attention, consistent review, and constant focus?

Passion is when you put more energy into something than is required to do it. More than just enthusiasm or excitement, passion is an ambition that is converted into action to put as much heart, mind, body, and soul into something as possible. Passionate leaders motivate and inspire their people to be the best they can be and put as much of their best selves forward as they can to achieve their goals. Passionate leaders can share their ambition with others and inspire them to go after the same goals. Simply put, passionate leaders and managers make a lasting difference.

> **Exodus 2:13** 13 *The next day he went out there again. Two Hebrew men were fighting. He spoke to the man who started it: "Why are you hitting your neighbour?" (MSG)*

Moses was passionate about the condition of his brethren so much so that he went out the next day, and when he encountered two Hebrew men fighting, he could not keep quiet and he, out of concern, raised his voice, "Why are you striking your companion?" This is not a rare one-time event but a regular multi-time effort. He just could not sit in the confines of his palatial home; his passion propelled him to his people.

Is your passion pushing you out of your 'pleasure zone' into what I call your 'pain zone'? Passion invariably pushes you into pain zones and inflicts agony, affliction, and aches. That is what passionate individuals do. That is what passionate individuals think. That is what passionate individuals choose: pain over pleasure. They are consumed by thinking about their passion and investing time doing what they need to do and are passionate about than doing what they want to do!

b. Passion Does Not Rest Despite Odds

Odds are an integral part of life, and the legacy builders are fully aware of this. So, when confronted by odds, you do not give up instead prepare for the best time, the best opportunity, and the best opening. And you know what? As you are prepared, when the opportunity shows up, when the time is right or when the opening is out, you can capitalize on your opportunities.

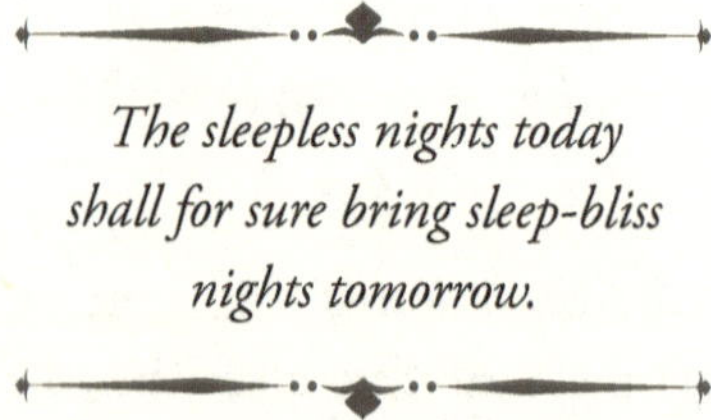

Passionate people spend sleepless nights pursuing their vision and purpose, and remember - the sleepless nights today shall for sure bring sleep-bliss nights tomorrow. What am I saying? Passion does not rest despite the odds. Moses, the scriptures say, went back the next day. He just couldn't sit in the comfort of his palace thinking, I have done my good deed for the people of Israel – I have squashed the enemy by taking his life. Now let me be comfortable. No, not Moses. His passion made him restless and propelled him back to his platform.

Your passion pushes you to your platform where you will get launched. Your platform in turn paves way for your prominence. Colossians 3:23 says, *"Whatever you do, work heartily, as for the Lord and not for men."*

c. Passion Finds Its Way, No Matter What

Thomas Edison may hold the record for the most failed attempts before finding success on one particular project. He tried and failed numerous times before creating a working light bulb. Entrepreneurs have come to know and love his response: "I have not failed. I recently discovered 10,000 methods that won't work." Albert Einstein is quoted as saying, "I tried 99 times and failed, but on the 100th time I succeeded." Moses experienced repeated failures in his attempts to liberate Israel nine times but he continued on until he succeeded. Passion is what keeps the fire burning even when darkness is at its darkest. Passion finds its way no matter what. What are you passionate about? How do you channel your passion? Find your passion and your passion will find you. More importantly, find your passion to live to your potential.

My Reflections...

My Response...

My Actions...

PRINCIPLE 11

You Will Experience a Fair Share of Gaps but Shall Find Your Strength

I would like to highlight three gaps that Moses struggled with and the coping strategies he was able to muster.

a. Lack Of Confidence

> Exodus 3:11-12 [11]*But Moses said to God, "Who am I that I should go to Pharaoh, and that I should bring the children of Israel out of Egypt?"* [12]*So He said, "I will certainly be with you."*

Often a feeling of inadequacy is the key contributor that pulls down legacy builders from achieving their full potential. Lacking confidence has devastating consequences, wherein you run the risk of losing out on the game plan God has crafted for you. Some have an inflated view of themselves and others have a deflated view. Both are colossal.

Legacy builder, are you underconfident? Are you like Moses saying, "who am I?" If that is your question today, this word is for you; "but I will be with you." This is the assurance that God provides you. This is the confidence which comes from above – a God-fidence – God-infused confidence; very few have the right kind of confidence – it is not over-confidence or under-confidence but the God-fidence; this is where God recognizes your strengths and your limitations – HE knows you through and through for He knitted you in your mother's womb and thus He says, "I will be with you." Regardless of how you feel; He assures you that He is with you.

At a practical level, how do you build God-fidence? You trust Him fully, take Him at His word and focus on one small thing at a time, get better at that one thing and move on to other areas; avoid focusing on multiple areas all at once and you shall grow in God-fidence.

b. Lack Of Competence

In a fast-paced world with a significant explosion of knowledge and the rapidly evolving spheres of science, the disruptions created by technology can be extremely formidable. The competence gap is real and is widening by the day. A global survey carried out by one of the top global consulting firms indicated that as high as 70% of graduate recruits hired in certain countries lacked the skills required to be successful in their jobs. Additionally, under 60% of the Boards were certain of the leadership capabilities of their CEOs to take their organisations to unchartered territories. The competence gap is real and often the lack of competence can be a potent threat to legacy builders.

> **Exodus 3:13** *Then Moses said to God, "Indeed, when I come to the children of Israel and say to them, 'The God of your fathers has sent me to you,' and they say to me, 'What is His name?' what shall I say to them?"*

> Exodus 4:10 10 *Then Moses said to the LORD, "Please, Lord, I am not a man of words (eloquent, fluent), neither before nor since You have spoken to Your servant; for I am slow of speech and tongue."(AMP)*

Moses was confronted with two competence gaps. One, "Now they might say to me, 'What is His name?' What should I say to them?" That is the gap of ignorance. This certainly is a serious issue in today's world. Unconscious incompetence and conscious incompetence are issues that many managers and leaders grapple with on an ongoing basis. With the advent of google and other search engines while the mechanisms for bridging the ignorance gaps have improved significantly the advances in technology and super specialisations keeps the ignorance gap quite high.

The second incompetence is to do with inexperience or lack of expertise. Moses said to the Lord, "Lord, I am not a man of words. I have never been." For he stammered, and it was difficult for him to speak. As a leadership consultant, I recognise the importance of communication; often communication is considered to be the threshold requirement for effective leadership. And Moses had neither the skill nor the expertise in speaking – from a worldly standpoint, he was a non-starter! Mark his words – I have never been a man of words. This implies that it was not a new problem but an old one. Like Moses, do you amplify your problem? Is the lack of competence that you are confronted with limiting you? Do you feel that there is no way to get around your challenges?

I would like to point you to God's response.

> Exodus 3:14 *God said to Moses, "I Am Who I Am"; and He said, "You shall say this to the Israelites, 'I Am has sent me to you.'"*

"Say to the Israelites, 'I AM has sent me to you.'" Your ignorance is met by His knowledge. Your incompetence is met by His competence. Further in chapter 4:

> Exodus 4:11,12 11 *Then the Lord said to him, "Who has made man's mouth? Who makes a man not able to speak or hear? Who makes one blind or able to see? Is it not I, the Lord?* 12 *So go now. And I will be with your mouth. I will teach you what to say."*

Your inexperience is met by His expertise. So hand over your inexperience or lack of competence into His hands. If you are worried today about your lack of experience or expertise – He says that He is aware of your lack of experience or expertise. Are you on the threshold of a greenfield project? Are you awaiting a change of role? Are you about to start a new venture and are intimidated by the uncertainties involved? He shall bridge that gap for you as you go about applying yourself wholeheartedly!

c. Lack Of Credibility

Credibility essentially is the extent of trustworthiness a person enjoys. In leadership, credibility plays a significant role. When credibility is eroded, leaders fall flat on their faces.

> Exodus 4:1-5 1 *Then Moses answered and said, "But suppose they will not believe me or listen to my voice; suppose they say, 'The Lord has not appeared to you.' "* 2 *So the Lord said to him, "What is that in your hand?" He said, "A rod."* 3 *And He said, "Cast it on the ground."*

So he cast it on the ground, and it became a serpent; and Moses fled from it. [4]Then the LORD said to Moses, "Reach out your hand and take it by the tail" (and he reached out his hand and caught it, and it became a rod in his hand), [5]"that they may believe that the LORD God of their fathers, the God of Abraham, the God of Isaac, and the God of Jacob, has appeared to you."

What do you have in your hand? – That is your vehicle for establishing your credibility

Moses had credibility issues. He was asked to consider what was in his hands. Often you look outside seeking ways to enhance your credibility. Here is a powerful lesson to look within. If you were to go searching for credibility elsewhere, you may be disappointed for it is external to you and does not last long. Looking at what you already have, is a good place to start building your credibility. What do you have in your hand? Moses had a rod and that was his tool to establish his credibility. What do you have in your hand? Is that a degree, a skill, a capability or expertise? Whatever it is – that is your vehicle for establishing your credibility. Mine it, leverage it, deploy it, and you will establish your credibility.

My Reflections...

My Response...

My Actions...

PRINCIPLE 12

Powerful Others May Not Subscribe to Your Vision; Progress, Nevertheless

Deference to powerful others in your life may prove advantageous but is often disadvantageous. You, like Moses, may encounter powerful others who do not value your vision, may place roadblocks on the way or even pull down your efforts. Your response to their actions will determine if you achieve what you are purposed to achieve or give in. I would like us to examine three key areas of dissent that you are likely to face as a legacy builder:

a. Powerful Others May Not Recognize The Anointing In Your Life

> **Exodus 3:1-5** 1 *Now Moses was tending the flock of Jethro*
> *his father-in-law, the priest of Midian. And he led the*
> *flock to the back of the desert, and came to Horeb, the*
> *mountain of God.* 2 *And the Angel of the* Lord *appeared*
> *to him in a flame of fire from the midst of a bush. So*
> *he looked, and behold, the bush was burning with fire,*
> *but the bush was not consumed.* 3 *Then Moses said, "I*
> *will now turn aside and see this great sight, why the*
> *bush does not burn."* 4 *So when the* Lord *saw that he*

turned aside to look, God called to him from the midst of the bush and said, "Moses, Moses!" And he said, "Here I am."

Exodus 3 provides an overview of Moses' encounter with GOD in the burning bush. That encounter changed Moses' entire outlook significantly. A divine encounter can have a significant impact on your life; transforming your position, transcending your experience, and transitioning you into a new phase of life that you never thought possible. The question is, do you have a burning bush experience? If you have not, I would urge you to seek that burning bush experience; for that changes you in fundamental ways. During the burning bush experience, Moses was touched in three distinct areas and experienced an anointing that may have relevance to your life today.

A divine encounter can have a significant impact on your life; transforming your position, transcending your experience, and transitioning you into a new phase of life that you never thought possible.

Genesis 4:2-4 [2]*So the LORD said to him, "What is that in*
your hand? "He said, "A rod." [3]*And He said, "Cast it on*
the ground." So he cast it on the ground, and it became
a serpent; and Moses fled from it. [4]*Then the LORD said*
to Moses, "Reach out your hand and take it by the tail"
(and he reached out his hand and caught it, and it
became a rod in his hand).

i. Rod: The rod in Moses' hand became the powerful conduit of God's power. It stands for direction, correction, and leadership. The rod in your hand provides direction to your people and is a symbol of correction and alignment. It points to the mantle of leadership in your life – a distinct anointing to bring leadership to your context – but this anointing may not be acknowledged by Pharaoh and others.

> **Genesis 4:6-8** [6]*Furthermore the LORD said to him, "Now put your hand in your bosom." And he put his hand in his bosom, and when he took it out, behold, his hand was leprous, like snow.* [7]*And He said, "Put your hand in your bosom again." So he put his hand in his bosom again, and drew it out of his bosom, and behold, it was restored like his other flesh.* [8]*"Then it will be if they do not believe you, nor heed the message of the first sign, that they may believe the message of the latter sign.*

ii. Hand: The word hand occurs 1290 times in the Bible. It signifies authority, authenticity and power. The hand of God was upon Moses and his hand became the channel of His power; that hand is upon you as you read these lines and with that hand, He seals you with His authority, anoints you with His authenticity, and crowns you with His power.

> **Genesis 4:** [9] *And it shall be, if they do not believe even these two signs, or listen to your voice, that you shall take water from the river and pour it on the dry land. The water which you take from the river will become blood on the dry land."*

iii. Water: Water occurs 722 times in the Bible. It signifies life, it symbolizes purification, protection, and palliation. When God used water as one of the signs to demonstrate His power, He perhaps indicated to Moses that the death of the Egyptian river Nile was to spark the life of the Israelis.

The point is that the anointing from GOD is so real, so tangible, and so powerful yet the so-called powerful may not recognize it. You know what – it does not matter – regardless of others recognizing your anointing, notwithstanding others accepting your authority, irrespective of others paying allegiance to the hand of God in your life – you have the anointing of GOD. As a legacy builder, you need NOT get the nod of the powers that are – if you have an encounter with the Omnipotent Power above all powers.

b. Not Heed The Command Of God:

> **Exodus 5:1-2** [1]*Afterward Moses and Aaron went in and told Pharaoh, "Thus says the LORD God of Israel: 'Let My people go, that they may hold a feast to Me in the wilderness.'* [2]*And Pharaoh said, "Who is the LORD, that I should obey His voice to let Israel go? I do not know the LORD, nor will I let Israel go."*

The world today refuses to recognize the GOD of ages, the world often shuns the God and the fear that should rightfully grip the people is not witnessed just like Pharaoh! The God of eternity does not spell terror in the minds of the so-called powers and they do not think of GOD as one who is to be revered. Do not be anxious, let not their stance wreak havoc in your life and send you scurrying in fear. Remember what happened to Pharoah; their audacity is short-lived, their arrogance will come to an end soon, and their animosity shall cease, for the Lord's anointing in you shall work its way to accomplish what you thought was impossible.

c. Not Recognise Humanitarian Considerations

> Exodus 5:7-8 7 *"You shall no longer give the people straw to make brick as before. Let them go and gather straw for themselves. [8]And you shall lay on them the quota of bricks which they made before. You shall not reduce it. For they are idle; therefore they cry out, saying, 'Let us go and sacrifice to our God.'"*

While considerable shifts have happened in the areas of philanthropy and corporate social responsibility is taking centre stage, and certain pockets have emerged more sensitive to the needs of others, a significant gap still exists in being empathic to the needs of the underprivileged or economically deprived. That this callousness exists in the more elite and higher rungs of society is saddening.

Moses experienced this firsthand in his interaction with Pharaoh, the king of Egypt. When asked to be released from servile servitude, Pharoah refused to offer raw materials but demanded the same level of output instead. This response is a classic illustration of the mindset of the world's powers, who harden their hearts and are oblivious to the plight of the poor and needy. The governments in many countries frequently appear to be working hand in glove with the wealthy and show little care for the plight of the poor while the rich get richer. In several instances, decisions appear to be illogical, ignorant, and plain indifferent to the plight of the lower strata of people. Pharaohs of today emerge in the fields of commerce and business and are engaged in pushing the divide between the haves and have-nots further. The absolute disregard for minimal wages in many parts of the country and beyond, the total indifference to the working conditions of those who work in dire unhygienic conditions, and the total lack of sensitivity to the basic needs of other human beings are telling.

Let not the indifference, inaction, or impudence of the world around detract you. Legacy builders ignore the actions of the so-called powers that are and continue to progress despite all odds to realise their life purpose. The message is clear – do not let the so-called powerful in your life dictate terms to you that are contrarian to your explicit life purpose.

My Reflections…

My Response…

My Actions…

– III –

David, the Dynamic King

David, the second king of the historic United Kingdom of Israel (c. 1035–970 BC), is said to have contributed to the creation of Israel as a country. Former shepherd David was well known for his love of God, his stirring Psalms and musical talent, his inspiring bravery and military prowess are legendary, and what is even more remarkable is that his descendant is Jesus of Nazareth in the New Testament. Like King Saul and King Solomon, David, a member of the tribe of Judah and the eighth and youngest son of Jesse, ruled for 40 years during what is frequently referred to as "The Golden Age" of Israel, one of the best and wealthiest periods in Israeli history.

David, an ordinary shepherd boy grazing his sheep in the wilderness had a distinct calling on his life which propelled him from the outskirts of the city to the centre stage. His was an amazing journey that bloomed into a narrative of struggles and more struggles intertwined with streaks of successes.

As you consider the life of David there are sterling lessons that you learn – from his early days, his growing up period, and his sunset years. I would like us to unravel 12 life principles that I believe are meant to guide, govern, and grace your life.

PRINCIPLE 13

It's Not Where You Come From, It's Where You Are Going That Matters

David was an ordinary shepherd boy who had no semblance of royalty. He was perhaps the least among the least. But David had cultivated the right spirit early in life and this took him from anonymity to celebrity status. Outlined below are three key elements that you are to be cognizant of:

a. Don't Begrudge Your Humble Beginnings

> 1 Samuel 16:11 *And Samuel said to Jesse, "Are all the young men here?" Then he said, "There remains yet the youngest, and there he is, keeping the sheep."*

David was the last of eight brothers. Thus, from a family hierarchy standpoint, he was at the top from the bottom. When Samuel the prophet came to visit the Jesse family, the father very proudly introduced his sons and David was not even considered to be in the reckoning to be showcased to Samuel. When Jesse was asked to bring his sons before Samuel, he had conveniently forgotten the existence of David! Thus, he was possibly considered insignificant by the older family members – the lowliest among the lowly individuals.

Further, he was a shepherd boy. Shepherding, 5000 or so years ago, was considered a lowly occupation, just as it is today. Thus, from a social perspective, he was from one of the weaker sections of society. In all, he had a very humble beginning. Bharat Ratna Dr. APJ Abdul Kalam, the famed Indian scientist turned President of India, is known to have humble beginnings. He is said to have studied under a streetlight and yet became the People's President of India.

Humble beginnings are God-shaped opportunities without the trappings of comfort to ensure you are well-prepared to take on the role God has predestined for you. Don't ever be sorrowful of your humble beginnings; take pride in them, speak of the lowly state you came from and highlight how He lifted you up. For He certainly will lift you as you surrender yourself fully unto Him. This is what David did. He was oblivious to the plans God had for him but gloried in His humble beginnings. Abraham was a man of humble beginnings, but he ended up as the father of many nations. David the humble shepherd boy grew to become the most loved king of Israel.

John Bunyan was born in England in the year 1628, "of a low, inconsiderate generation," in his own words, "came from obscurity." But while in jail for his faith, Bunyan wrote *The Pilgrim's Progress*. Some estimate that *The Pilgrim's Progress* is possibly the second-widest-read book in the world. Your beginnings may be simple, but your end can be sublime.

Remember the scriptural injunction, *And whoever exalts himself will be humbled, and whoever humbles himself will be exalted.* - (Matthew 23:12).

Don't whine about your humble beginnings – they are not a handicap but a help from above, they are not a step-down but a channel of a step up, it is not a limitation but a means to liberation.

Don't whine about your humble beginnings – they are not a handicap but a help from above, they are not a step-down but a channel of a step up, it is not a limitation but a means to liberation. So dear friend, if you think you have a humble beginning and are concerned about your antecedents, cheer up – you are in good company, for Jesus Christ was born in a manger, but He grew to influence the world like no other.

b. Don't Bewail Your Tough Life Experiences

> 1 Samuel 17:34-37 [34]*But David said to Saul, "Your servant used to keep his father's sheep, and when a lion or a bear came and took a lamb out of the flock,* [35]*I went out after it and struck it, and delivered the lamb from its mouth; and when it arose against me, I caught it by its beard, and struck and killed it.* [36]*Your servant has killed both lion and bear; and this uncircumcised Philistine will be like one of them, seeing he has defied the armies of the living God."* [37]*Moreover David said, "The LORD, who delivered me from the paw of the lion and from the paw of the bear, He will deliver me from the hand of this Philistine."*

David, when tending his sheep, was confronted with a range of challenges and life-threatening circumstances. He encountered a lion and a bear. He was not frightened by these wild animals, but he vanquished them with his skill and grace. There could be tough lion-like enemies that are vying for your life, or the bear market conditions possibly seeking to destroy your life savings, and you are going through a truly challenging period. But you know what was David's response to tough challenges in life? He was absolutely confident that He will be preserved despite the most ardous of circumstances.

Don't be frightened by those tough life experiences, for they are avenues for God to demonstrate His power to overcome the giant Goliaths in the future. As you meet lions and bears today, remember they are the preparation ground for destroying those mammoth Goliaths you will face tomorrow!

The human brain cannot comprehend the negative. Let me conduct an experiment with you. Are you ready? Keep your eyes closed and focus on the wall in front of you. Now, I would like you to follow carefully and do what I would ask you to do: Don't think of a big dark buffalo. How easy was that? Very often the reinforced dogmas when put in the negative negates itself, e.g., I can't do this versus I am going to keep doing this – it is such a blessing to convert things into the affirmative. When you tell the captain of the ship – don't hit the obstacle, they will hit the obstacle. Because what they are doing is focusing on the obstacle. If you focus on the obstacles all you will see is the obstacles. See beyond the obstacles and you will see the hand of God crafting a beautiful future.

c. Don't Bemoan Your Wilderness

When David's brothers were in the thick of the action, David was relegated to the wilderness to tend the sheep. When the family celebrated special events or festivals, everyone was invited but he was out in the wilderness. Remember when Samuel came to Jesse's house to offer a sacrifice unto the Lord, all his brothers were present with the exception of David. Do you bemoan that you are not where the action happens? Do you bemoan your time away from the family doing that less important work? What is the wilderness you are going through?

There is no better place to strengthen your muscles, deepen your faith, and widen your perspective than the wilderness!

Whatever your wilderness is, remember David had an equally bad wilderness experience if not more intensive. Jesus, the Son of man had to encounter wilderness where He was tested before He was trusted. Your wilderness is your test and once you are tested you will be trusted. Why? Because the wilderness brings with it challenges that are important components of shaping your faith and when your faith is refined, it is ready to take on greater challenges. Don't bemoan your wilderness but bless them for there is no better place to strengthen your muscles, deepen your faith, and widen your perspective than the wilderness!

My Reflections...

My Response...

My Actions...

PRINCIPLE 14

Opportunities Are Emissaries to Channel Your Growth to Gigantic Proportions – Grab Them

Opportunities abound for those who have trained their ears to pick them up. Invariably opportunities come in the form of challenges. Every challenge opens a window of opportunity. If you are sensitive to sense those opportunities and invest in exploring them, you can leverage the opportunity to your advantage.

> **1 Samuel 17:8-10** 8 *Then he stood and cried out to the armies of Israel, and said to them, "Why have you come out to line up for battle? Am I not a Philistine, and you the servants of Saul? Choose a man for yourselves, and let him come down to me.* 9 *If he is able to fight with me and kill me, then we will be your servants. But if I prevail against him and kill him, then you shall be our servants and serve us."* 10 *And the Philistine said, "I defy the armies of Israel this day; give me a man, that we may fight together."*

Here is Goliath, a giant who is over nine feet tall and well-built, setting forth an open challenge saying, "I defy the armies of Israel this day; give me a man, that we may fight together." David was an errand boy on a mission to take food to the fighter brothers. And he overheard this gloating of Goliath. What do I learn from this?

First, opportunities come in the form of challenges. When confronted by challenges, you have the option to rise and take the challenge head-on, or you have the option to let the challenge go by. It is your response to emerging challenges in your world of work or life that determines if you will make a mark or not in this world. If you nurse ambitions of being a hero, or a spark, you should be willing to take up those challenges. David was willing to take the challenge, and it paved the way for his name to become a household name across Israel.

Secondly, where you currently are, has no semblance of where you could be. Why do I say that? David was an errand boy carrying the ration for his brothers. But the opportunity came by, David leveraged that opportunity and became the King of Israel. What was it about David that enabled him to use the opportunity to his advantage? Three key prerequisites aided David in his pursuit. Let us take a look at these.

a. Overriding Zeal

> **1 Samuel 17:24,26** 24*And all the men of Israel, when they saw the man, fled from him and were dreadfully afraid.*
> 26*Then David spoke to the men who stood by him, saying, "What shall be done for the man who kills this Philistine and takes away the reproach from Israel? For*

who is this uncircumcised Philistine, that he should defy the armies of the living God?"

We get a peek into David's zeal here. What do you pick up from these words of David?

i. David had a sound understanding of himself.

ii. He had a clear understanding of the enemy, Goliath.

iii. He could not tolerate that a heathen should defy his armies.

When you are consumed by that overriding zeal you do not see the circumstances but see beyond the circumstances.

He did not see the stature of the enemy or listen to stories of the formidable challenges set by the giant or pay heed to the fear that gripped the men of Israel. All these pointed to an impossible situation. There are times that the external appearances of the enemy may be formidable, the reaction of others may dampen your spirits, and the emerging scenario may sap your energies – but not for David, he was unmoved by all the drama that went around. He was filled with a zeal that the Lord's armies were being defied and that was not acceptable to David. Are you zealous? What are you zealous about? Does the zeal for the Lord consume you? Remember Psalms 69: 9, 'the zeal for your house consumes me'. When you are consumed by that overriding zeal you do not see the circumstances but see beyond the circumstances.

b. Overwhelming Conviction:

The second pre-requisite that David nurtured was an overwhelming conviction. David said, "The Lord, who delivered me from the paw of the lion and from the paw of the bear, He will deliver me from the hand of this Philistine." I would like you to consider the conviction he had. He did not say He may deliver or He can deliver; David said He WILL deliver me from the hand of the Philistine. You know what? For the Israeli soldiers and the people of Israel, the problem they encountered was gigantic and therefore induced fear, but for David, the Philistine was merely another giant, as he had encountered many giants in the wilderness and therefore was energised by faith in the Living God who can destroy yet another giant. That is what conviction does – conviction confronts the challenges head-on and leverages its power to find pathways to achieve significant outcomes. If you have been struggling in an area for a long time and have been in a quest for a breakthrough – check your conviction, and once you fix the conviction the conversion will follow. An overriding zeal undergirded by a sound knowledge of where that zeal emanates from is a sure way forward.

A group coaching exercise for the MD and his immediate reports of an MNC's senior leadership team was requested of me several years ago. The leaders were all poker faces in a domineering environment. The room's air conditioning was high. My responsibility as the facilitator was to mentor the group and help them become more effective as a unit. I was uneasy because the atmosphere wasn't especially cosy. I drew inspiration from several previous occasions when I had facilitated similar sessions and received standing ovations from the audience. I felt more assured as a result and was strengthened in my spirit. I took a few deep breaths, murmured a word of prayer, and then jumped right into the session with a lot of energy. The whole team was energised, and the MD thanked me profusely for a session that had been so enlightening. The session as a whole would have been jeopardised if I had given in to my fear and the intimidating audience. However, getting stronger in the conviction allowed for a smooth transition.

c. Overcoming Adversaries/ Adversities

David had a fair share of adversaries and adversities. Being a legacy builder does not insulate you from adversities or isolate you from adversaries. You will encounter both adversaries and adversities. But overcoming adversaries of smaller intensity prepares you to meet the adversaries of greater intensity in your life. Who are those adversaries or what are those adversities that you are contending with? Is it a love for money? Love for fame? The need to laud yourself over others? The desire to consider yourself as always right and others as wrong? A sense of pride that bloats your ego so much that you cannot see the difference between the shades of grey. Whatever those adversaries, make a conscious effort to defeat them. That is the starting point. Recently, my wife disagreed with my stated opinion during a conversation. She had done it before, and I handled them amicably. However, this time, my ego was bruised, and I harboured resentment and gave her the "silent" treatment. My silly ego was exposed to me during my reflection, and I kissed and made up with my wife. Dear legacy builder, do you nurture aspirations to spark others' lives? You aspire well. Do you aspire to be the sunshine in your vicinity – you desire very well. Equally ensure you nurture an overriding zeal, nourish an overwhelming conviction and negate everything that comes in the way of overcoming those adversaries that seek to destroy your wellbeing and if you do, you should be well on your way to leveraging the opportunities that come your way.

My Reflections…

My Response…

My Actions…

PRINCIPLE 15

Your Anointing Paves the Way for Your Advancing

That David was anointed to be king was not common knowledge. To many, he was just an ordinary shepherd whose place was in the wilderness with the sheep, and he was accorded no credence higher than that of a mere shepherd boy. Why do I say that?

> 1 Samuel 17:28 *Now Eliab his oldest brother heard when he spoke to the men; and Eliab's anger was aroused against David, and he said, "Why did you come down here? And with whom have you left those few sheep in the wilderness? I know your pride and the insolence of your heart, for you have come down to see the battle."*

After being anointed king, David was sent out to his brothers with food for them and his brothers berated him. What do we learn from here?

i. Others may not acknowledge where you are in the trajectory of your life.

ii. There may not be any significant change in your place of work or the people you hobnob with after your designated promotion.

iii. Others may not treat you with deference.

On the contrary, you may be spoken to harshly, and looked down upon by your family and friends. If that is where you are today, I have good news for you. David the anointed king experienced all these in his life. But you know what? No one could deny that he was the anointed king. No one can take it off you; that you are anointed with a specific plan, for a distinguished purpose. I would like to highlight three distinct components of the anointing – 3 Cs:

a. Choice

Choice is the highlight of the anointing in your life. You are chosen for a designated purpose. David, you did not choose to be the king, none of your family members chose you to be the king – they passively resisted your becoming the King, but GOD chose you. Remember 1 Peter 2: 9, *"But you are a chosen race, a royal priesthood, a holy nation, people for His own possession, that you may proclaim the excellencies of Him who called you out of darkness into His marvellous light."*

Further, John 15:16 says, *"You did not choose me, but I chose you and appointed you so that you might go and bear fruit — fruit that will last — and so that whatever you ask in my name the Father will give you."* This is an important truth to bear in mind. You are chosen and appointed for a reason. Do you know the reason for your existence, the reason you have been chosen, the reason for your position in this cosmic world? You did not happen by accident, it was not some bizarre chance that you are where you are; you have been chosen – allow that to sink into you. The choice has to do with the Chooser rather than the chosen, the Chooser has the prerogative to choose in accordance with His good pleasure. Thus the fact that you are chosen is a privilege, an honour and a distinct advantage that is to be celebrated with humility and gratitude.

b. Calling

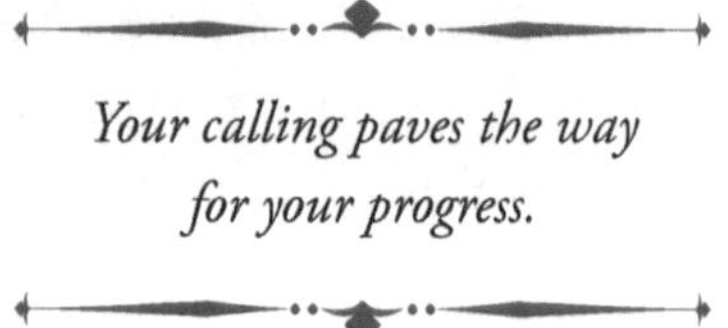

Your calling paves the way for your progress.

David had a distinct calling in his life. He came to terms with His calling rather quickly. Why do I say that? After his anointing to be the king he recognized his calling and confronted the giant Goliath. What do I learn? Your calling paves the way for your progress.

> **1 Corinthians 1:26-29** 26 *For you see your calling, brethren, that not many wise according to the flesh, not many mighty, not many noble, are called.* 27 *But God has chosen the foolish things of the world to put to shame the wise, and God has chosen the weak things of the world to put to shame the things which are mighty;* 28 *and the base things of the world and the things which are despised God has chosen, and the things which are not, to bring to nothing the things that are,* 29th *at no flesh should glory in His presence.*

The above verses are powerful and revealing. It provides the essence of the 'calling'. Earlier we spoke of the calling of Abraham that propelled him to venture out into uncharted waters. Here you find a fresh dimension of that calling. Often the call is not offered to the sophisticated but the simple, not the eloquent but the empathic, not the erudite but the eager. David, you may not be tall in stature or equipped to be a man of war mighty like your brothers, you may not be wise like other wise men BUT you are called by GOD and that is what counts. You know "the Who" of the calling – God is the one who called you. You also need to know why you are called. 1 Thessalonians 4:7 says, *"For God hath not called us unto uncleanness, but unto Holiness. The Lord who called you is faithful to lead you till the end of times and grant you the grace for holiness."*

c. Crowning

> 1 Samuel 16:13 *Then Samuel took the horn of oil and anointed him in the midst of his brothers; and the Spirit of the LORD came upon David from that day forward. So Samuel arose and went to Ramah.*

> 2 Samuel 2:4 *Then the men of Judah came, and there they anointed David king over the house of Judah.*

> 2 Samuel 5:3 *Therefore all the elders of Israel came to the king at Hebron, and King David made a covenant with them at Hebron before the LORD. And they anointed David king over Israel.*

Here is an insight: David was anointed to be king when he was possibly 15 years old, as we read in 1 Samuel 16:13. But, in 2 Samuel 2:4, he was crowned as king of Judah at the age of 30, but it was in 2 Samuel 5:3, he was crowned as the king of Israel. There is a time gap between your anointing and you're crowning. Dear leader, you are anointed but the manifestation of the anointing may not be evident immediately. It took 15 long years for David to be crowned and 22 years to be crowned fully. The time lag between the promise and the realization can be multiple years, but the crowning shall happen. The wait can be long, tedious, and demanding, but wait patiently for your time and your advancement shall come in due course. Often you lose heart, feel demotivated, and are tempted to give up, but the crowning is on its way in line with your choice and calling.

My Reflections...

My Response...

My Actions...

PRINCIPLE 16

Fastrack Does Not Mean a Journey without Fumes

Upon His anointing, David experienced an unusual grace and favour that soon saw him rising the charts. I would like to consider three facets of David's life that could very well be the reality of anyone on a fast track to growth.

a. Gathering Momentum

> 1 Samuel 18:5 *So David went out wherever Saul sent him and behaved wisely. And Saul set him over the men of war, and he was accepted in the sight of all the people and also in the sight of Saul's servants.*

David was a maverick, and any task assigned to him became an easy chore for him to accomplish. He was gathering significant momentum functionally, professionally, and hierarchically. Whatever mission Saul sent him on, David was so successful that Saul gave him a high rank in the army. This pleased all the troops, and Saul's officers as well. He was the rising star, the talk-of-the-town, the cynosure of all eyes. You may be a rising star in your work context, whatever you touch may turn into gold, your professional charts may consistently be going North, you are possibly the preferred choice for any greenfield project, you consistently ace all the projects, and your professional trajectory is gathering momentum.

That is a clear sign of you being a rising star. "The world is wide, and I will not waste my life in friction when it could be turned into momentum," said Frances E. Willard. Momentum calls for focus and excellence bundled together. As you hone your skills, you learn continually and grow constantly. You will gain momentum and progress in every facet of your life. Have you plateaued in your life? Have you reached a point where progress seems to be impossible any longer? Check your momentum. I had the privilege of consulting with the richest man in the country and his leadership team. One thing that he was excellent at was building and maintaining momentum and he tasked his leadership team to do that and the results are evident for all to see.

Gathering momentum calls for perhaps a set of apparently contradictory skills; a sharp focus on the objective and the flexibility to accommodate the requests emerging from the people who are to be shepherded towards the objectives. Do you bring that sharp focus to your goals and at the same breath bring an evolved flexibility to ensure people are aligned towards the objectives? If not, you may want to invest in these skills.

b. Growing Popularity

> 1 Samuel 18:6-7 6 *Now it had happened as they were coming home, when David was returning from the slaughter of the Philistine, that the women had come out of all the cities of Israel, singing and dancing, to meet King Saul, with tambourines, with joy, and with musical instruments.* 7 *So the women sang as they danced, and said: "Saul has slain his thousands, And David his ten thousands."*

David was growing in popularity. When popularity increases, it brings with it a fair amount of enemies or frenemies. The popularity of David vis-à-vis Saul is stark. When the men were returning home after David had killed the Philistine, the women came out from all the towns of Israel to meet King Saul singing and dancing, with joyful songs and timbrels and lyres. 7 *…as they danced, they sang: "Saul has slain his thousands, and David his tens of thousands."* The women attributed a 900% higher standing to David as compared to Saul. Remember, they came to meet Saul, but here they were praising David!

When your popularity grows, when your Youtube likes increase, when your following on Twitter doubles, when your videos on TikTok go viral, when your ascent is higher than your superiors and you are seen as more popular, how will you handle it? Also, if you were to spin it, when someone else gets more popular than you, how do you handle it? The way you handle popularity or the lack of it will determine how you weather the testing times ahead. For, testing times will certainly come your way. If you are over the top and popularity gets to your head or if you are down in the dumps with the lack of it, you have a problem at hand. Abraham Lincoln said, "Avoid popularity if you would have peace," and William Penn is said to have quoted, "Avoid popularity; it has many snares and no real benefit." Perhaps a worthwhile question to ask yourself is, what compromises have you made or are willing to make to achieve popularity?

c. Gruesome Antagonism

> 1 Samuel 18:8 *Then Saul was very angry, and the saying displeased him; and he said, "They have ascribed to David ten thousands, and to me they have ascribed only thousands. Now what more can he have but the kingdom?"* [9] *So Saul eyed David from that day forward.*

Popularity invariably breeds antagonism, jealousy, and enmity. David experienced that vitriolic enmity. Saul was very angry; the refrain, "Saul killed his 1000s and David his 10,000s," displeased him greatly and that pushed him to attempt to take David's life. There could be those that do not like your progress. There could be those that look for opportunities to belittle you, snub you or even take your life. If you experience the antagonism of your colleagues or superiors or people in your social circuit, how do you react?

An acquaintance of mine who used to play badminton with Mukesh Ambani in the Bombay Gymkhana had this to say; "Mukesh could never take losing a game, and if he lost a game he would hold a grudge against his opponent." David for no fault of his found Saul antagonistic towards him. What should be your response? Ensure the Lord is with you – which is what Saul recognised – that the Lord was with David and he met more success.

Consider Psalm 91:7, *"A thousand may fall dead beside you, ten thousand all around you, but you will not be harmed."* That is the assurance you have. Do you know why? In verse 9, we read the answer: *"Because you have made the* L*ORD*, *who is my refuge, Even the Most High, your dwelling place."*

You don't need to be afraid of the antagonism you experience in the world, for no antagonism can strip you of your legacy.

So dear leader, you don't need to be afraid of the antagonism you experience in the world, for no antagonism can strip you of your legacy.

My Reflections...

My Response...

My Actions...

PRINCIPLE 17

Find a Friend Who Stays Closer Than a Brother

Proverbs 27:9 *"...A sweet friendship refreshes the soul."*

In a highly materialistic world finding good friends has become a major challenge. Time and good friends get valuable as you become older, but their importance when you are young cannot be understated. He who finds a good friend finds a friend for life. From a legacy standpoint, good friends enable you to leave a legacy that counts; for they are with you through thick and thin and know the pluses and minuses which in turn enables them to fine-tune you into a better person and a legacy builder. David had a great friend, Jonathan, and their friendship lasted a lifetime. I would like to present three facets of David and Jonathan's friendship that may script a few lessons for you to capture.

a. Friendship Beyond Social Class

1 Samuel 18:16-17 [16]*So Jonathan made a covenant with the house of David, saying, "Let the LORD require it at the hand of David's enemies."* [17]*Now Jonathan again caused David to vow, because he loved him; for he loved him as he loved his own soul.*

David was part of the shepherding community, and Jonathan was the crown prince; hence rightful heir to the throne of Israel. But Jonathan and David were thick friends. The class divide did not come in the way of their friendship. In a day and age where the social divide was as pronounced as any other age, David and Jonathan's friendship crossed all social borders and their love was genuine – 24-carat gold love. You get a glimpse of their love in the above quote from 1 Samuel 18: *And Jonathan had David reaffirm his oath out of love for him because he loved him as he loved himself.* In a world where friendships are formed in the light of class and caste considerations, here are David and Jonathan crossing those concerns to love genuinely. How many friends do you have that are from a different class or a different caste or a different age-group? David and Jonathan nurtured their relationships fully conscious of their different genres.

> **1 Samuel 20:41** *As soon as the lad had gone, David arose from a place toward the south, fell on his face to the ground, and bowed down three times.*

Their friendship did not diminish the honour they showed each other. Clearly, David was the smarter, surer one of the two, but we find David bowed before Jonathan three times and they kissed each other with a holy kiss. Remember Romans 12:10 - *Be devoted to one another in love. Honour one another above yourselves.* Here is a perfect example of honouring the other above oneself. Often within friendship, you tend to take the other person for granted. You think it is all right to pull the other person down, and as they see familiarity breeds contempt and that contempt invariably comes in between the friendship. Proverbs 17:17 says *"A friend loves at all times."* Do you love your friends at all times? Perhaps this is a gentle reminder to love as never before. Dr. APJ Abdul Kalam said, "If you really want to look handsome, give your hand to some and you will automatically look handsome."

b. Friendship With God At The Centre

> 1 Samuel 20:23 *"And as for the matter which you and I have spoken of, indeed the LORD be between you and me forever."*

What I found particularly interesting is the number of times Jonathan refers to GOD in their conversation. At least six times in chapter 20. When bosom friends meet, the conversations invariably meander towards unsavoury issues and often the guard is let down, the language is more explicit, and God is the last thing on their minds. With David and Jonathan, this was not the case. The Lord was at the centre of their friendships. Is God at the centre of your friendships? David and Jonathan were completely aware that they were in the presence of the Lord and whatever they did they had the audience of the ONE there with them, and that was the basis of their friendship. Have you endeavoured to have God as an active participant in your deliberations and laughter within your friendships?

c. Friendship That Is Willing To Go Beyond

> 1 Samuel 20:4 *So Jonathan said to David, "Whatever you yourself desire, I will do it for you."*

David and Jonathan's friendship was willing to go beyond. Jonathan said to David, "Whatever you want me to do, I'll do for you." This is truly an unparalleled friendship. How much are you willing to do for your friends? Invariably there is a line clearly drawn between what you will do for your friends and where you will stop. But here we find a no-holds-barred kind of friendship. What is even more interesting is that Jonathan knew from his father that as long as David was alive neither he nor his kingdom will be established, we read in:

> 1 Samuel 20:31 *"For as long as the son of Jesse lives on the earth, you shall not be established, nor your kingdom. Now therefore, send and bring him to me, for he shall surely die."*

and yet Jonathan treasured his friendship. Often you encounter friendships where as long as the friend is placed lower than you are, or the friend is earning lesser than you or your friend does not get the vied promotion, and you received that advancement, you are happy. Not so with Jonathan.

> 1 Samuel 23:16-17 16 *Then Jonathan, Saul's son, arose and went to David in the woods and strengthened his hand in God.* 17 *And he said to him, "Do not fear, for the hand of Saul my father shall not find you. You shall be king over Israel, and I shall be next to you. Even my father Saul knows that."*

In the above context, Jonathan reaches out to help David find strength and shares something beautiful – you will be king of Israel and I will be second to you. This is truly the icing on the cake. He did not burn with jealousy or share his father's sentiment of destroying the perceived enemy, but he was filled with joy to strengthen his friend. How far do you genuinely celebrate the success of your friends? Do you know that there is a powerful mystery in blessing your friends? In Job 42:10 we find that *"after Job had prayed for his friends, the LORD restored his fortunes and gave him twice as much as he had before."* What a powerful word!

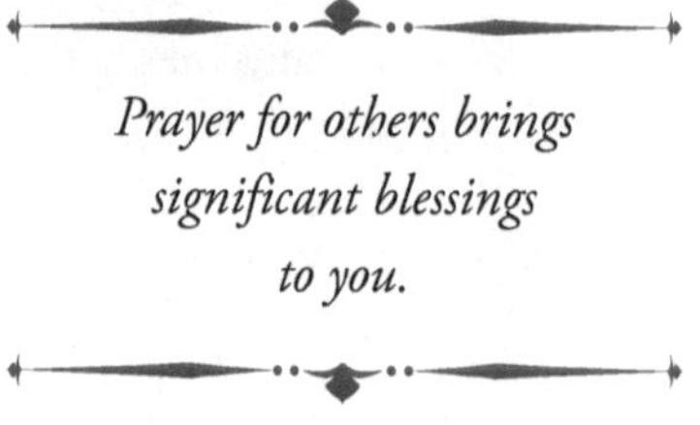

Prayer for others brings significant blessings to you.

Job prayed for his friends, and He restored fortunes twice over. Do you experience a lack in your life? Do you find that your efforts are not yielding the progress they ought to? Try this recipe. Try praying for your friends earnestly, and you shall experience a breakthrough. I had a buddy in school, Santhosh who was concerned about my wellbeing and wrote to the prayer tower seeking prayer support for me, and I was blessed and he was doubly blessed – he migrated to Australia and is now a flourishing neurosurgeon there. Prayer for others brings significant blessings to you.

My Reflections...

My Response...

My Actions...

PRINCIPLE 18

Return Good for Evil

In a world where evil is returned for good, the innocent are harmed and people hold themselves back from standing up for their rights, legacy builders are made of a different genre. What makes legacy builders stand out from the rest of the crowd is their penchant for operating at a significantly higher level than those in the rest of the crowd. I would like to present three lessons from the life of David for us to tap into.

a. Respect Beyond Reason

David demonstrated respect for Saul that borders on deference. The respect came from the fact that Saul was anointed by the Lord to be the king of Israel. This was reason enough for David to respect Saul. Despite the numerous instances, in which Saul breached the relationship of a king and subject, a superior and subordinate, a military leader and his general, and more importantly a father-in-law and son-in-law, David did not let that breach come in the way of his respect for Saul. In a world that operates on the premise, "Give respect and take respect," and where the dictum, "you scratch my back, I scratch yours," is deeply seeded in the way we conduct business and interactions, here is David exercising a great sense of respect for Saul. Unmerited but heartfelt respect for the ordained is the hallmark of a legacy builder.

What is particularly interesting is that the respect for Saul that David exercised defies logic or reason. Saul was out to destroy David and did not lose an opportunity to kill David – yet on David's part, he did not lax his respect for Saul.

> 1 Samuel 24:4-7 [4]*Then the men of David said to him, "This is the day of which the LORD said to you, 'Behold, I will deliver your enemy into your hand, that you may do to him as it seems good to you.'" And David arose and secretly cut off a corner of Saul's robe.* [5]*Now it happened afterward that David's heart troubled him because he had cut Saul's robe.* [6]*And he said to his men, "The LORD forbid that I should do this thing to my master, the LORD's anointed, to stretch out my hand against him, seeing he is the anointed of the LORD."* [7]*So David restrained his servants with these words and did not allow them to rise against Saul. And Saul got up from the cave and went on his way.*

The above narrative gives you an insight into the mindset of David. He was conscience-stricken that he had cut off the hem of Saul's garment, and his words of remorse give you a glimpse of the heart of David. He said, "The LORD forbid that I should do such a thing to my master, the LORD's anointed, or lay my hand on him; for he is the anointed of the LORD."

We live in a time where we are rather lenient with the way we speak about those in leadership; political, religious or social. The number of Youtube videos that seek to tear those in leadership into shreds abounds by the day. The question is where is the respect for those anointed into leadership positions? Do you demonstrate respect for the Lord's anointed? If there have been slips, this is an opportune time to bring about course correction in your thoughts, words or deeds.

b. Repeated Offences Forgiven

David is a man made of different mettle. He seems to defy the saying, "once bitten twice shy". Saul was a repeat offender, and he turned himself into a sworn enemy of David. Saul hated the very grounds David walked – he burnt with enmity, animosity, and hostility towards David. He hated David's guts, David's popularity, David's anointing, David's strength, and the hand of GOD upon David. In effect, Saul hated everything about David. Every effort of his to get close to David including making him his son-in-law was with an explicit intent of destroying David. He made no secret of his hatred for David and he made multiple attempts to kill David. Not once, not twice, not thrice but on eight occasions, including two instances when he tried to pin David to the wall with a spear. Despite all these attempts David was spared.

As you bring positivity to the negativity around you, the positive rubs off on the negative environment and positivity is birthed.

Dear leader, do you have someone in your life or work who hates you to the core – that he or she would like to see you decimated? As you endeavour to be like David and do not retaliate, you will heap live coals on their bosom, for your behaviour will not make sense to them, your responses will be alien to their psyche and they will be foxed as to how to relate to you. Your kindness, goodwill, and graciousness will have a greater impact on them than any retaliatory behaviours. Do you know why? As you bring positivity to the negativity around you, the positive rubs off on the negative environment and positivity is birthed. Forgiveness has the effect of a balm. It soothes the nerves, cleanses the hurt and band-aids the broken spirit. It does not merely relieve the forgiven but liberates the forgiver.

Oh! I love this man, David. He had his sworn enemy who tried to kill him eight times being in his grasp to do as he pleases with him – and David let him go! What an amazing restraint and strength of character. Truly a remarkable benchmark in human relationships. My wife is exceptional in that she holds no grudges. There were times when an ex-manager made life so difficult for her for no fault of hers and given the illogicality of the scenario, I had asked her to quit her job but she persisted and was unusually good towards her manager. Her ex-boss was shown the door and thereafter she became so courteous towards my wife. Do you hold enmity against your enemies? Or are you willing to forgive their offences?

c. Resilience That Counts

David consistently bounced back. Imagine his maturity to be able to spring back despite the repeated attempts to devour his spirit, destroy his body and decimate his mind. It was as though nothing could keep him down. He had the tenacity to spring back despite the most arduous of circumstances, repeated attempts on his life, and diverse efforts to obliterate him. The number of Psalms he had penned is descriptive of his spiit that bounced back. That is resilience that counts. Are you resilient? If not, perhaps you need to cultivate the resilience of David. That is a hallmark of a legacy builder.

My Reflections…

My Response…

My Actions…

PRINCIPLE 19

Fight Your Battles in the Spirit

During David's period as king, he frequently engaged in battles and wars to expand his lands and had to deal with opponents regularly. Today, we experience spiritually what David went through physically. I would like to investigate David's strategy and military tactics to understand how he waged those wars and became renowned as the best king Israel has ever had. You can draw inspiration from the following three lessons from David's approach to fighting his battles.

a. Reliance On God To Fight Your Battles

David was a seasoned warrior. Right from a young age, he fought with lions and bears in the wilderness, and in his adolescent years he destroyed the giant Goliath and further obliterated 200 Philistines in his growing up years. Thus, he is no ordinary man of valour. He had perhaps the skillfulness of a skilled fighter and the strategic insight of a strategist of acclaim. Yet, in the scriptures we find David doing something significant before every war. Do you know what he does?

> 1 Samuel 23:1-2 [1]*Then they told David, saying, "Look, the Philistines are fighting against Keilah, and they are robbing the threshing floors."* [2]*Therefore David*

> *inquired of the* Lord, *saying, "Shall I go and attack these Philistines?" And the* Lord *said to David, "Go and attack the Philistines, and save Keilah."*

I marvel at this amazing relationship he enjoyed with God. This is just one instance when he inquired from the Lord. The scriptures record nine inquiries he made of the Lord. Here lies the secret of David's strength. Don't get me wrong – David was a mighty man of valour; he had accomplished great military feats singlehandedly. But he did not rely on his physical strength, mental skill, or psychological prowess BUT he inquired of the Lord. I learn three fundamental lessons from this:

i. He awarded pre-eminence to God in his life.

ii. He did not rely on his past accomplishments to craft his future strategies.

iii. He heard from God before he progressed on his mission.

With his capabilities and evolved strengths, David's first port of call was the Lord God. Often when encountered with a tricky work situation or a problem to solve, your mind wanders into the past to validate your approach and secure your plan of action for the future. Invariably you zero in on the people who have perhaps supported you with similar situations in the past. While seeking human assistance appears logical to people, it did not seem logical to David. He sought the Lord. For he recognized that human wisdom has its limitations.

Human insight is largely governed by past experiences or at best extrapolations. While they have their merits – they fall significantly short of the dynamic environment and the ensuing changes. Thus, you need a more incisive insight and forward-looking foresight that is beyond human capabilities. One that is perhaps far more sophisticated than the most advanced Artificial Intelligence (AI) that processes multiple billion bytes of information in nanoseconds to give your output. That is where God comes into the picture – for He never is wrong! AI can go wrong, and machine learning may have bugs, but He never goes wrong. Do you seek divine intervention when encountering trying or difficult situations in your life? It could be to embark on a new project, maybe a contentious conversation you need to engage in, or it could be something to do with a difficult problem that you are called to address – whatever your situation is, there is merit in inquiring of the Lord.

You need a more incisive insight and forward-looking foresight that is beyond human capabilities.

You frequently look back to your prior successes to gain inspiration, but David didn't. His prayer to the Lord was wise because he didn't know what tactics would be effective for the obstacles he would face in the future based solely on how he had previously dealt with the enemy. So, putting your trust in the Lord's omniscience is potent as you tap into the vastness of the wisdom of God for managing your life issues. Do you rely on God more than anything else to combat your life's circumstances and challenges?

b. Refuse To See The Might Of The Enemy

David never saw how big the enemy was, how well-endowed the enemy's frontlines were, how mighty the enemy was. The challenges you face may be formidable, the gravitas of the circumstances you go through may be daunting, and the complexity of the tests you are called to face may be intimidating but, like David, refuse to see the might of the enemy. In life, like in war, when you see the enormity of the enemy you are contending with, you are very likely to feel small, insignificant, and weak. But when you see the weakness of the opponent, the frailties, fragilities, and flaws of the adversary, you are more than likely to devise effective mechanisms to overcome the adversity.

Several years ago, I was leading a high-stakes client engagement with a million-dollar company who were investing significantly in leadership development. One of the big 4 consulting companies was in the fray and offered a solution to the client that appeared very convincing. The client awarded part of the project to the big 4 consulting firm. There was pressure from the client to adapt our approach to align with this big 4 competition. I saw a fundamental flaw in their approach, stood my ground and convinced the client to measure the effectiveness of our outcome vis-à-vis the big 4. The results were significantly in our favour. Knowing who you are contending with and their flaws, ensure you curate, accentuate, and leverage offerings that speak to your strengths.

When you build on your strengths fully aware of the enemy lines, the scriptural verses become alive as in Deuteronomy 28:7 *"The LORD* will cause your enemies who rise against you to be defeated before you. They shall come out against you one way and flee before you seven ways." Further, Isaiah 54:17, *"No weapon that is fashioned against you shall succeed, and you shall confute every tongue that rises against you in judgment. This is the heritage of the servants of the LORD* and their vindication from me, declares the *LORD."* Additionally, Exodus 23:22 *"But if you carefully obey his voice and do all that I say, then I will be an enemy to your enemies and an adversary to your adversaries."*

Isn't that awesome? The Lord, your God shall be an enemy to your enemy. Your sworn enemy is the devil, and the Lord shall be an enemy against the devil on your behalf and you shall obtain victory over all your enemies as David did and recorded in 2 Samuel chapter 8. The Philistines, the Moabites, the Arameans, the Edomites, the Ammonites, and the Amalekites. These enemies shall never find their hands above yours! Hallelujah!

c. Refreshed By God

> 1 Samuel 30:3-4,6 [3]*So David and his men came to the city, and there it was, burnt with fire; and their wives, their sons, and their daughters had been taken captive.*
> [4]*Then David and the people who were with him lifted up their voices and wept, until they had no more power to weep.* [6]*Now David was greatly distressed, for the people spoke of stoning him, because the soul of all the people was grieved, every man for his sons and his daughters. But David strengthened himself in the LORD his God.*

David was greatly distressed because his family was taken captive, the city was burnt down, and the men were talking about stoning him. Adverse situations such as these are bound to come your way. There may be occasions where your family members are suffering from illness for several weeks or months, a business that you built and cultivated from scratch may cave in, and people who adored you may turn antagonistic – these could very well be possible realities.

In the face of such trying circumstances, David found strength in the LORD, his God, and was refreshed by God. Jeremiah 31:25 says, *"For I will satisfy the weary soul, and every languishing soul I will replenish."* Further, Philippians 4:6,7 states when you are confronted with the might of the enemy, *"Do not be anxious about anything, but in everything by prayer and supplication with thanksgiving let your requests be made known to God, And the peace of God, which surpasses all understanding, will guard your hearts and your minds in Christ Jesus."*

No matter how difficult the circumstances you go through are or how troubled you are because of the distress you are going through, there is a refreshing from the Lord that you can tap into!

My Reflections...

My Response...

My Actions...

PRINCIPLE 20

Slip Does Not Mean Slain

The saying even an elephant may slip is so true. We see numerous examples of stalwarts you hold in high esteem slip, fall and fail. The business world has numerous examples of great business giants who failed miserably. Walt Disney's Animation company failed, Henry Ford's The Detroit Automobile Company & Henry Ford Company failed, Akio Morita's rice cooker manufacturing company failed, James Dyson was rejected over 5000 times, and Colonel Sanders' recipe was rejected several times. But their failures did not detract these business giants. They did not languish in their failings but gathered themselves and went about reaching great heights. Walt Disney established the Walt Disney Company which makes an average revenue of $30bn yearly. Henry Ford rose from his failures and established the Ford Motor Company which became a huge success. Akio Morita went on to co-found Sony Corporation. James Dyson established the globally best-selling vacuum cleaner – the Dyson vacuums, and Colonel Sanders went on to set up the brand KFC which is synonymous with crispy chicken.

These giants, who are the best among the best crumbled and failed, and so did David. He had a lapse that was a defining moment in his life and became the reason for some of the most cited Psalms. I would like to examine what led up to the fall of David and how David went about his slip to draw three life lessons:

a. Be Where You Are Required To Be

> 2 Samuel 11:1-2 [1]*It happened in the spring of the year, at the time when kings go out to battle, that David sent Joab and his servants with him, and all Israel; and they destroyed the people of Ammon and besieged Rabbah. But David remained at Jerusalem.* [2]*Then it happened one evening that David arose from his bed and walked on the roof of the king's house. And from the roof, he saw a woman bathing, and the woman was very beautiful to behold.*

Being in the wrong place at the wrong time can never bring the right outcomes at the right time.

Being in the wrong place at the wrong time can never bring the right outcomes at the right time, but it can have colossal consequences. As we traverse through the pages of history, there are several examples of people being in the right place at the right time have had significant positive outcomes and similarly being in the wrong place at the wrong time has had several negative consequences.

David was required to be at war. Instead, he chose to stay back and enjoy the comfort provided by his position in the hierarchy. When you are required to lead from the front but choose to stay back, there is a slide that has already happened. Are you where you are required to be, at this point? Both physically and metaphorically.

If you are not in the place that you should be, you will end up in a place that you shouldn't be! That is a warning sign that you possibly are headed for trouble. I was in Mumbai with my wife for a weekend, and there was an option for me to stay back or go to Mahabaleshwar, a hill station along with my wife where she operated from. I could have stayed back in the comfort of my Mumbai waterfront home and enjoyed the luxuries that it offered but I prioritized being with my wife over being in Mumbai on my own, in the comfort of my home and you know what? I went to the hill station that weekend and I experienced a myocardial infarction in the early part of the week and received immediate medical attention. Had I continued in Mumbai, I possibly would have succumbed to the three blocks, two of them 90%!

The question that you need to ask yourself is, are you where you are required to be? Often being in the wrong place, at the wrong time is sufficient for a downward dip in your life. Like David, are you caught up in the wrong place? If you are, get back to the right place lest you be ensnared.

b. See What You Are Required To See

The eyes are the window to your soul said William Shakespeare and eyes most often are the receptacles of virtue and vice. I remember a chorus my grandmother taught me when I was a kid. "Two little eyes to see God, two little ears to hear Him speak." That is a powerful little chorus that many of us may have sung, but unfortunately, the passage of time has possibly eroded the message that the little chorus had. That is what happened with David. He had his eyes in the right place, as he sang in Psalm 141:8, *"But my eyes are toward you, O God, my Lord; in you, I seek refuge; leave me not defenceless!"*

And further in Psalm 119:18, *"Open my eyes, that I may behold wondrous things out of your law,"* and Psalm 25:15, *"My eyes are ever toward the Lord, for he will pluck my feet out of the net."*

But something seems to have gone wrong. His eyes began to wander as he was in the wrong place at the wrong time, and his eyes that revelled in the beauty of the Lord began to take in the beauty of another man's wife, and that spelt the death knell for his soul.

The question is what content are your eyes taking in? If you watch the wrong content, invariably your actions will turn wrong. Remember Job in Job 31:1, *"I made a covenant with my eyes not to look lustfully at a young woman."* Have you made a covenant with your eyes? If you haven't you will end up like David and will slip and fall!

c. Do What You Are Required To Do

Once David compromised on his stand with his eyes, the natural consequence was a compromise on his actions. Once compromised, invariably you end up compromising multiple times. David did not do what he rightfully ought to have done – come back into his house and fall on his knees and cry out unto God and say, 'Lord I am sorry I sinned with my eyes. Let me not transgress against you.' Had he done that, history would have scripted a different story. But David slipped and slumped. He allowed his sensual pleasure to get the better of him and did what he was not supposed to do and that brought a set of devastating consequences that he had to live with, including the loss of his son.

When you fall and fail, know that you need not stay fallen or be a failure. You can take corrective actions to extricate yourself from failure. The saying failure is not final is perhaps true in this context more than ever before. Consider, the reasons for failure and find ways to overcome it. Dear leader, do you do what you are required to do? Or, like David have you allowed what you are not to do to be done? If you have done what you should not have done – like David, you have an opportunity to turn your face unto the Lord and cry out as in Psalms 51:1-2, [1] "*Have mercy on me, O God, according to your unfailing love; according to your great compassion blot out my transgressions.* [2] *Wash away all my iniquity and cleanse me from my sin.*"

My Reflections...

My Response...

My Actions...

PRINCIPLE 21

Subscribe to a Higher Code

David as a man is perhaps like many of us; he had a fair share of successes and failures, streaks of excellence and patches of lapses, and a set of clear strengths and confounding weaknesses. That he was struggling with certain aspects of his life is amply evident in the pages of history. This makes him human. With some major blunders and several minor breaches, his life was by no means impeccable or beyond reproof. Yet we read that he was testified of as a man after God's own heart in Acts 13:22. The question is why?

What made David a man after God's own heart with all his failings, foibles, and faults? Let me set this in context. It is important to note that God sees very differently from what man sees. God saw David as a Man after His own Heart – in contrast with the man's perception in 1 Samuel 17: 28 - *Now Eliab his oldest brother's anger was aroused against David, and he said, "Why did you come down here? And with whom have you left those few sheep in the wilderness? I know your pride and the insolence of your heart, for you have come down to see the battle."* What a contrast!

Man invariably sees very differently from God. So what do you learn from this? Man will invariably perceive differently, very differently from God. However, the perceptions of man do not matter, but the point of view of GOD is what matters. Are you one who suffers from faulty perceptions of the people around you? Have you been misunderstood by others? Misinterpreted by others? Misrepresented by others? In the final analyses, as long as God sees your heart and it is sparkling clean with all its intentions, initiatives, and innovations that is all that matters.

I would like to set forth three reasons why David was seen as a man after God's own heart, and that gives you hope that you can strive to be a man or woman after God's own heart.

a. A Hallowed Reverence For The Sacred Writ

David thrived on the scriptures. His love for the Word is evident in the Psalms he scripted and the life he lived. Remember Psalm 119:105 - *Your word is a lamp to my feet and a light to my path and further in*, Psalm 1:2 - *You get a glimpse of how he delighted in the law of the Lord and meditated on His word day and night.*

What is your flashlight as you go through dark passages of life? What is your torchlight as you navigate through tough decisions in your work?

That reverence for the word of God is what set him apart as a king from others like Saul. David had an awesome understanding of the scriptures not merely at an intellectual level, but he truly believed it with all his heart. For example, Deuteronomy 32:35 states - *vengeance is mine and recompense; their foot shall slip in due time, for the day of their calamity is at hand and the things to come hasten upon them.*

That scripture ensured that he did not take Saul's life when it appeared as though Saul was handed to him on a platter. That is the conviction he had. What a wonderful spirit is that! A heart that takes God at His word and never moves away from His word. What is your flashlight as you go through dark passages of life? What is your torchlight as you navigate through tough decisions in your work? What is your reference point as you encounter challenges with the truth? David subscribed to a higher code and that ensured he left a lasting legacy. What moral code do you subscribe to?

b. A Hyper-Sensitive Conscience Eager To Make Amends

To err is human is the adage and David was human and thus he made some big blunders. But what made David stand apart from most others is that he had developed a highly sensitive conscience that was seared when he transgressed and he sought to make amends. Psalms 51 presents the state of mind of David after he committed adultery with Bathsheba and got her husband killed. Psalm 51:3 – *"For I know my transgressions and my sin is always before me."*

He was conscious of his sin, and his sin was always before him. It is as though the wickedness he had committed ate into him so much so that he could not take his mind off it. That is a sensitive conscience. An interesting anecdote about Ratan Tata, the chairman Emeritus of the Tata empire is shared. When in the U.S., he fell in love with a girl and was keen to marry her. But, he had to return to India owing to his grandmother's ill health. The girl could not join him as her parents refused to send her to India due to the Indo-Chinese war. Ratan came to India and the girl married someone else but Ratan kept his promise and never married. Once an interviewer asked, "Why did you keep your promise even after the girl left?" He is reported to have said, "That's when the pious significance of a promise is tested – when a person leaves." What a benchmark he had set for himself!

Doing the right thing even when you can get away with doing the wrong thing is truly the right thing to do. And should you slip into not doing the right thing – repenting from and restitution of the wrong into the right is a hallmark of a man or woman after God's own heart.

c. A Heart Of Gratitude Overflowing Into Worship

> 2 Samuel 6:13-14 13 *And so it was when those bearing the ark of the LORD had gone six paces, that he sacrificed oxen and fatted sheep.* 14 *Then David danced before the LORD with all his might; and David was wearing a linen ephod.*

David's worship was a no-holds-barred kind of worship. In 2 Samuel 6: 14, we read David danced before the LORD with all his might. I like the expression here – with all his might! David danced before the Lord with all his might, perhaps overflowing with gratitude for the hand of God in his life – this was worship – God honouring – God-focused worship. How do you worship God? Are you more concerned about who is watching you? How you are being captured on video, or are you out and out focused on God – where He is the ONLY focus during your time of worship – worship that is oblivious of the surroundings?

There were men and women, his subjects and orderlies, but David was not mindful of these– his attention was rivetted on GOD, and to his scornful wife he said in 2 Samuel 6:21, *"it was before the Lord."* No one mattered to him, he was not playing to the gallery, he was interested in the audience of ONE. Is your worship targeted towards the audience of One?

My Reflections...

My Response...

My Actions...

PRINCIPLE 22

Find Your Spiritual Anchor

When you think of David, what comes to mind is the array of Psalms written by him and he is often referred to as the Psalmist David rather than king David. He was a worshipper first and then a king. His allegiance to the spiritual was far more deeply seeded in him than the allegiance to other goals in his life. Several Psalms written and sung by David give a glimpse of David's quest for the spiritual and how much he treasured God in his life. That David was such a great worshipper is one key reason that he achieved the esteemed position of being called a man after God's own heart. I would like to present three highlights of David's spiritual life that in turn paved the way for him to leave a formidable legacy.

a. Ensconced In His Presence

David had an in-depth, unquenchable, uncontrollable quest for the spiritual. His spiritual longing and craving resulted in his seeking God. *"As the deer pants for streams of water, so my soul pants for you, O God. My soul thirsts for God, for the living God,"* he said in Psalm 42:1. Further, he had an evolved understanding of God's presence. In Psalm 139:7 he said, *"Where can I go from Your Spirit? Or where can I flee from Your presence?"*

We often find leaders who do not recognize the presence of God. They go about their actions as though the spiritual dimension is non-existent. As though God is a fiction, a non-entity. Not so with David; his words are rich with meaning – where can I flee from your presence?

That tells me he was practising the presence of God. The Latin word 'Coram Deo' meaning living in the presence of God is what David subscribed to. When you recognize you are in the presence of GOD every moment of your life, you cannot but be in awe of Him and when you are in awe of Him all the allures of the world will turn awful to you. That is the magical power of His presence, for it significantly decreases the potency of the world and its attraction to you, as you bask in His presence.

Remember Psalm 91:1 - *"He that dwelleth in the secret place of the Highest shall abide under the shadow of the Almighty."* When you live in His presence every moment, you are under the shadow of the Almighty God. That shadow ensures no harm can touch you. And that, in turn, springs up a stream of worship unto the Lord. Further in Psalm 16:11 he says, *You will make known to me the path of life; In Your presence is fullness of joy; In Your right hand, there are pleasures forever.*

There are many today whose lives are lived without joy. Do you know the reason? They don't live in the presence of the Lord. Are you living a life without joy? Check if you have moved out of the presence of the Lord. And Psalm 51:11 tells you that your sins can cast you away from His presence. Have you allowed your sins to cast you away from His presence? Come back into His presence and raise that conscious awareness of

His presence, and you shall experience the pleasures of His right hand.

b. Enthralled By His Magnificence

David was besotted by the Lord's magnificence. In Psalm 8:1 he said, *Yahweh, our Lord, how magnificent is Your name throughout the earth! You have covered the heavens with Your majesty.*

In a day and age where it is fashionable to use the name of the Lord as a swear word, here is David in awe of the name of the Lord. He was not only in awe of the Lord's name, in Psalm 92:5 he says, *How magnificent are Your works, Lord, how profound Your thoughts!*

> *Time spent in awe of His presence has a significant rub-off effect. It translates you from the 'side-lines' to the 'centre stage', it takes you from 'off the screen' to being 'in the frame', it turns you into a person with 'no say' to a person of 'substance' who shapes outcomes.*

He is in awe of the Lord's works and His thoughts. Have you taken time to be in awe of the Lord's works and His thoughts concerning you? Jeremiah 29:11 says, *For I know the thoughts I think toward you, says the Lord, thoughts of peace and not of evil, to give you a future and a hope.*

The Lord's thoughts toward you are worthy of awe. For He has seen you in your lowly state and has set you apart to sit with princes – isn't that marvellous? I know of a director of one of the top organizations in the country who during his younger days would spend hours closeted in the prayer room, worshipping God. Time spent in awe of His presence has a significant rub-off effect. It translates you from the 'side-lines' to the 'centre stage', it takes you from 'off the screen' to being 'in the frame', it turns you into a person with 'no say' to a person of 'substance' who shapes outcomes. That is the magnificence of the Lord.

c. Enjoying His Courts

In a world where people shy away from anything to do with God or the things of God, where the mention of the temple of God is explicitly scorned or shunned, king David had a completely different take. In Psalm 27:4 he says, *"One thing I have asked from the Lord, that I shall seek: That I may dwell in the house of the Lord all the days of my life, To behold the beauty of the Lord And to meditate in His temple."*

The only thing he asks of the Lord earnestly is that he dwells in the house of the Lord, not one day, not on Sunday or Saturday, but ALL the days of his life. Do you seek to go into the house of the Lord – would you love to be in His courts every day? Is that your desire? If it is, then that is a sure sign of a deep spiritual quest. When you are in His courts, you are inspired by the awesome God, and He fills your heart with songs of hope, fills your mouth with songs of praise and fills your mind with songs of worship. And when you worship God, something happens to you, in you and through you; you close your eyes and open yourself to God, you still yourself in His presence and know He is God, and you lose track of time as you clock time with God!

My Reflections...

My Response...

My Actions...

PRINCIPLE 23

Your Past is No Predictor of Your Future

There are times when you become a prisoner of the past, allowing the past to dictate your future. While the past does play a role in shaping the present and the present plays a role in securing the future, often the role of the past is glorified. There are innumerable examples of leaders who have broken loose of the inhibitions of the past and have carved out a progressive future for themselves and others. Invariably most legacy builders have had to contend with a past that is not particularly rosy. David, the legacy builder cum history maker did not have a very distinguished past. I would like to consider three contexts of David and draw lessons from his life as you go through the journey of building your legacy.

a. From Obscurity To Being Outstanding, From Insignificance To Significance

Like most leaders who grow to prominence and visibility, David also started his life in obscurity. To the outside world, he was a non-entity. Even within his family, he was viewed as one of not much value. When others have no great expectations from you, when your near and dear ones don't have great confidence in you, when your teachers don't have great hopes pinned on you, invariably you end up having no great expectations for yourself. It is a psychological phenomenon; remember when in school, one teacher saw a spark in you and said that he/she sees great potential in you and stated his or her expectations of you? What did it do? It spurred you, and you did all that you can to meet that expectation.

However, in the case of David, he had no legitimate expectations from his parents or his family or friends. He was truly and simply a lad clothed in obscurity. But you know what? David did not let others' view of him come in the way of the expectations He had of Himself based on His experience with God. Here is the first learning. Dear leader, your experience with God can significantly alter your expectations of yourself. Bakht Singh was an affluent Indian Sikh who lived a wayward life in Canada. When he had an encounter with God and experienced him, his expectations of himself changed significantly, and he transformed from a wayward lad into a man who found his way forward and in turn became an apostle of peace to his community and India at large.

Building your expertise, when you are in obscurity ensures you win the limelight when you are on centre stage.

When you have a life-touching experience, you are re-configured to respond to the world differently and that re-wiring ensures you engage in exposure-seeking, expertise-building and experience-gathering endeavours. Why do I say that? In the wilderness, David, unlike other shepherds did not stay in the confines of the safe territory. He sought exposure to the territories of the lions and bears and encountered them. That exposure in turn allowed him to encounter Goliath. It also pulled him out of the confines of obscurity to his being recognized as an outstanding fighter.

What do I learn from this?

i. When you are obscure - Use your time to your fullest advantage and your exposure will fill you with confidence to contend with the Goliaths of the world.

ii. When in the wilderness, David built his expertise; he perhaps was engaged in equipping himself with the shooting skills – shooting with stones – so much so that his expertise came in handy, and with a sling and stones, he brought the giant down. You know what? If you want your life to turn significant from insignificance, you will have to encounter giants and overcome them. Building your expertise, when you are in obscurity ensures you win the limelight when you are on centre stage!

iii. Experience gathering; experience is a key component to success. Research by one of the top consulting firms found that in the near term, experience more than compensates for lack of competence. Are you investing sufficiently in gathering the requisite experience – if you do, your experience will pave the way for your significance.

b. From Shepherding Sheep To Shepherding A Kingdom

David the shepherd was happily shepherding a few sheep in the wilderness. While shepherding the sheep, he invested his body, mind, and spirit in ensuring the sheep were safeguarded against the attacks of wildlife. He was completely unaware of his mission in life. You, like David, are possibly involved in your world oblivious of your mission in life. But if you, as David, will give yourself fully to doing what you are called to do *"as unto the Lord"* (Colossians 3:23) that will set you up for progress. When you do all that you do as though you do it for Him! His shepherding skills stood him in good stead when he transitioned into shepherding the kingdom. The scale, size and shape of his operations increased a million-fold as he moved from shepherding his sheep to shepherding his kingdom, but he had the wherewithal as He did what He did unto the Lord. The classical verse captured in Luke 16:10 presents this powerfully, *"He who is faithful in what is least is faithful also in much, and he who is unjust in what is least is unjust also in much."*

Whatever the size of your operations is today, it does not determine what it can be tomorrow. Know that it is not the magnitude of your ability but the attitude in your availability that is important.

c. From A History Sheeter To A History Maker

David's past was nothing to rave about, his antecedents were ordinary, his occupation was ordinary, and his claim to shame was adultery and murder, and thus he could very well be branded a history-sheeter. As you look at yourself today, do you find yourself like David with no great credentials to write home about? Well, the history-sheeter turned into a history-maker! David made history when Jesus Christ was born in the lineage of David! Romans 1:3 reads, *"Concerning His Son, who was born of a descendant of David according to the flesh."* That is the power of God that can transform you through and through – that your latter days shall have no semblance to the former days.

My Reflections…

My Response…

My Actions…

PRINCIPLE 24

Provide Leadership That Counts

David as a leader has spelt out several power-packed lessons to draw upon. I would like for us to consider key leadership lessons from his life that I believe are relevant for evolved and emerging leaders. Let me take the liberty of using the acronym LEADER to drive home these lessons for you to appreciate, appropriate, and apply.

L – Of Leader Is To Do With Leading From The Front

David consistently led from the front. He was not one to cower behind whether it was Goliath who he had to face, or the Philistines that he routed in 2 Samuel 5:17-25. There are times a leader ought to lead from behind no doubt, but there are other times when the leader ought to lead from the front and David did that well. The advantage of leading from the front essentially was –

There are times a leader ought to lead from behind no doubt, but there are other times when the leader ought to lead from the front.

i. He was in touch with the pulse of his people. He knew the sentiment of his front line, and that is powerful information to take informed calls.

ii. He was aware of the ploys of the enemy firsthand which enabled him to change tactics to overcome the enemy. Remember him pretending to be insane in 1 Samuel 21:1

iii. He was on the ground to make decisions on the spot that changed the course of outcomes. Are you leading from the front when you are required to?

E – Empathic To The Core

Empathy is a key differentiator between a leader who leads and a leader who leads effectively; for often the harder elements – the intellectual horsepower, the strategic insight, and the business acumen are amply available with leaders, what is not perhaps as evolved is the softer elements such as empathy. David was highly empathic.

> **2 Samuel 23:16-17** [16]*So the three mighty men broke through the camp of the Philistines, drew water from the well of Bethlehem that was by the gate, and took it and brought it to David. Nevertheless, he would not drink it but poured it out to the* LORD. [17]*And he said, "Far be it from me, O* LORD, *that I should do this! Is this not the blood of the men who went in jeopardy of their lives?" Therefore he would not drink it.*

Let me paraphrase this: the war with the Philistines was at its thickest. David longed for water and said, "Oh, that someone would get me a drink of water from the well near the gate of Bethlehem!" So three men who overheard the king say these words broke through the Philistine camp, drew water from the well near the gate of Bethlehem and brought it back to David. But he refused to drink considering the water as the blood of the men who risked their lives. That is empathy. Imagine the impact of his action of throwing that water to the ground on those three strong men and the millions who heard of that incident. They were hitched to him for life. That is the power of empathy. Are you empathic to your followers?

A – Adversity Tolerant

David faced numerous adversities, several attempts on his life by the king he regarded, many insults from his brothers he called his own, and numerous slights from his family members whom he doted on. The innumerable challenges he faced – the death of the child (2 Samuel 12: 15-31), the death of Amnon (2 Samuel 13:1-39), his son Absalom's conspiracy to overthrow him (2 Samuel 15:1-37)… the list goes on. But what made David distinct was he consistently overcame those adversities with amazing faith and redoubled determination.

The number of Psalms he sang is a testament to his tolerance. Psalm 9:9 - *"And Jehovah is a tower for the bruised, A tower for times of adversity."* Psalm 59:16-17 - *"I sing of your strength, And I sing in the morning of your kindness, For you have been a tower to me, And a refuge for me in a day of adversity."* Psalm 23:4 - *"Even when I walk through the darkest valley, I will not be afraid, for you are close beside me."* That is David's mantra to overcome adversity. Are you adversity tolerant?

D – Depth Of Conviction

A hallmark of a leader is that (s)he has an unshakeable conviction to overcome the impossible, override the implausible or overrule the improbable. In a world that is given to convenience, legacy builders go by convictions. They are willing to forego their convenience and are guided by their deep-rooted convictions. Legacy builders do not see the size of the problem but see beyond to the solution of the problems.

When encountering challenges, leaders bring the power of their conviction to the fore to ensure the impossible is made possible. David in his context went by convictions rather than convenience. Goliath was a formidable challenge – his stature, his size and his standing sent shivers down the Israelite army. But David used a different lens. He was convinced that the uncircumcised visible giant is no match for the invisible God and that turned the tables and changed the landscape completely.

> 1 Samuel 17:45-57 45 *Then David said to the Philistine, "You come to me with a sword, with a spear, and with a javelin. But I come to you in the name of the LORD of hosts, the God of the armies of Israel, whom you have defied.* 46 *This day the LORD will deliver you into my hand, and I will strike you and take your head from you. And this day I will give the carcasses of the camp of the Philistines to the birds of the air and the wild beasts of the earth, that all the earth may know that there is a God in Israel.* 47 *Then all this assembly shall know that the LORD does not save with sword and spear; for the battle is the LORD's, and He will give you into our hands."*

Here you get a glimpse of his conviction; "You come against me with sword, spear, and javelin, but I come against you in the name of the LORD Almighty, the God of the armies of Israel, whom you have defied." And in verse 47, his conviction is so strong – "All those gathered here will know that it is not by sword or spear that the Lord saves; for the battle is the Lord's, and he will give all of you into our hands." You know what, conviction eats capability for breakfast! When your conviction is strong, you overcome the enemy – with ease!

E – Exemplary Attitude

As a leader, you are required to make tough calls, grapple with difficult decisions, and take uncomfortable actions. Invariably when you make those tough calls, you will have dissenting voices. Your attitude, when confronted by voices of dissent, determines if you are a mediocre leader or a mature leader. In 2 Samuel 16, we have an account of David being called names by Shimei, son of Gera who levelled curses, pelted stones, and insinuated that the Lord had punished David. When David was asked, "Why should this dead dog curse my Lord, the king? Let me go over and cut off his head."

> **2 Samuel 16:11-12** 11 *David then said to Abishai! "Leave him alone; let him curse, for the Lord has told him to. It may be that the Lord will see my distress and repay me with good for the cursing I am receiving today."*

David did not seek revenge but got into a reflective mode. When others throw those stones at you, do you throw them back at them or do you take those bitter pills and allow God to minister to you? I had a friend who falsely accused me of wrongdoing in an august gathering of key stakeholders of an organisation; a part of me wanted to retaliate – I could have retaliated and "put him in his place" but I resisted the strong urge and let that go. When many came to me and said, "why didn't you give it back to him?" or "I would not have taken that from him," you know what my response was? I said I chose to follow the higher path that Jesus chose. How is your attitude to the wrong committed against you?

R – Radically Different

David as a leader was a radical, and he was radically different from Saul his predecessor. Whether it is their disposition or declaration, behaviour or being, impact or influence, they were distinctly different. Saul was cruel and David was benevolent; Saul was vicious and David was repentant; Saul sought praise from men but David was keen to please the Lord; when Saul made those blunders, he rebelled against God whereas when David encountered his heinous crime, he was remorseful and turned to God to seek forgiveness; Saul had the Holy Spirit taken from him whereas David prayed that the Holy Spirit would never be taken from him; Saul died a tragic death and David died a righteous death. A leader has to be radical and radically different from others. Are you radical for God? Are you radically different from others?

My Reflections...

My Response...

My Actions...

– IV –

Daring Daniel – Destiny Changer

Daniel's (6th century BC) life is riddled with the mystical and the magical. Nothing is known of his parentage, though he seems to have been of royal descent (Daniel 1:3); he was brought captive to Babylon (as part of the first expulsion of the Jews in about 605 B.C.) and was given the name Belteshazzar (1:6-7). Among the best Jewish youngsters, Daniel was chosen to receive training for a position in King Nebuchadnezzar's court. Daniel attained positions of authority within the Babylonian and Persian empires after being given the ability to interpret dreams by God.

Daniel, the young Hebrew boy, showed incredible promise and wisdom well above his years and King Nebuchadnezzar was drawn to him. Due to his talent, he quickly rose through the ranks to acquire the most sought position in the king's court. Daniel's colleagues and other top authorities tried to catch him doing anything wrong since they found his notoriety annoying. Because of his excellence, Daniel was able to fend off the jealous courtesans' attempts to overtake him and established himself as the nation's go-to expert. While his life was not always a bed of roses, and he had to deal with some terrible misfortunes, he did not succumb to them and instead used them to advance and leave a lasting legacy. Let's deep dive into his life to draw six principles for you to build on as a legacy builder.

PRINCIPLE 25

Walking through Adversity is an Opportunity to Advance

Daniel was comfortable in the region of Judah, his home town. Out of nowhere, his world is rocked. War can be terrifying and the recent Ukraine-Russia war is a testament to the number of lives that have been devastated and the resultant global displacement. Young Daniel lived a cushy comfortable life without any cares of the world. That changed in a moment without any warning! He possibly was separated from his parents and his siblings and was taken captive. Being a captive of war can be a difficult experience. Your freedom is curbed, your rights are severed, and your privileges are taken away from you. This can be a very challenging situation to be in. His world must have come crumbling down – suddenly orphaned, whisked away from the confines of his home to a strange country far from home. He was in the heat of adversity. So what does that teach us? I would like to present below three lessons:

a. Adverse Circumstances Are Crafted For A Greater Purpose

> Daniel 1:1-2 [1]*In the third year of the reign of Jehoiakim king of Judah, Nebuchadnezzar king of Babylon came to Jerusalem and besieged it.*

> Daniel 2:46 *Then King Nebuchadnezzar fell on his face, prostrate before Daniel, and commanded that they should present an offering and incense to him*

You think of adversity as restricting, making you powerless, losing control over your environment which can be frustrating, to say the least, but more importantly, adversity triggers a lone syndrome. You are isolated and insulated, and even the closest of your relatives and friends suddenly appear to be distant. It is not because they want to distance themselves, but adversity spins a story that distances you from them, and you can feel like a fish out of water. Daniel experienced all that. But you know what? It was that adversity that opened doors that he never explored, created avenues that he never considered, and revealed possibilities that he never imagined. He had King Nebuchadnezzar falling prostrate before him – a rather unusual thing for a king to do!

Invariably in the face of adversity, the initial reaction is that of fear and the ensuing action is to flee; while it is natural, it perhaps is not optimal for predominantly fear is crippling, and fleeing may clip your wings; some take ambiguity in their stride, some flounder in the face of adversity and some thrive in the backdrop of calamity. Be calm when calamity strikes, be astute when adversity hits, be agile when ambiguity comes by for neither the 'ants in the pants syndrome' nor a 'spate of criticisms' can wish away the reality of the situation; stay calm, take a considered approach, review all the variables and then decide the best course of action – remember, haste makes waste so be still and know He is God. Psalm 46:10 - *Be still, and know that I am God: I will be exalted among the heathen, I will be exalted in the earth.*

Adversities may very well be God's emissaries for reflection, restitution, and restoration. When you are encountered by the storms of life, when you find the song in your lips disappearing, and when you experience the squalls in life, be sensitive to the redirection. It points to when you come against strife in life. Be aware that it may raise you to the next level; for no storm shall befall you, no squall shall bend you, and no strife shall bind you that is not common to man/woman, and therefore distil the messages they bring and direct your attention to converting your adversity into your advantage.

> 1 Corinthians 10:1 [3]*No temptation has overtaken you except such as is common to man; but God is faithful, who will not allow you to be tempted beyond what you are able, but with the temptation will also make the way of escape, that you may be able to bear it.*

So what do you do when confronted by adversity? You call out to Him first, incline your ears to His voice next and ensure you do His bidding thereafter; for when He is called He answers with the best way forward, when you incline your ears, you hear Him speak and when you respond to His bidding; He has your being covered and secured. Jeremiah 33:3 says *"Call to Me, and I will answer you, and show you great and mighty things, which you do not know."* That is a promise for you to tap into as you go through adversity.

b. Circumstances Turning From Bad To Worse Does Not Mean Divine Absence

> Daniel 1:2 *And the Lord gave Jehoiakim king of Judah into his hand, with some of the articles of the house of God, which he carried into the land of Shinar to the house of*

his god; and he brought the articles into the treasure house of his god.

I would like you to consider the regressive deterioration of the circumstances surrounding Daniel. Not only was Judah besieged by Nebuchadnezzar, Jehoiakim king of Judah was given into Nebuchadnezzar's hand, Nebuchadnezzar further desecrated the house of God and carried the holy articles into the treasure house of his God! Additionally, Daniel was not only taken captive, but he was also tempted to do things that went against his grain. A constant step-by-step slide in his life. Can that happen to you? The answer is yes.

A needle prick is often necessary for the medication to flow through, and so does a dash of the unknown that allows you to tap into your creative genius to get around the discomfort.

When the unknown shows up to disrupt normal life, when the unspecified crops up to distort day-to-day living, when the unidentified turns up to disarray your way of life invariably, you are likely to feel aggrieved, agitated and aggravated. Don't let exasperation exacerbate you, don't let the irritation infuriate you, and don't let annoyance turn you apoplectic. Remember, a needle prick is often necessary for the medication to flow through, and so does a dash of the unknown that allows you to tap into your creative genius to get around the discomfort. He allows no trial to overtake you that He does not provide for a way.

In the throes of affliction, amid ailments, in the heat of adversity; seek His face, call unto Him, wait on Him to reach out in His mercy to remedy your body, renew your mind and restore your soul; for no bodily suppression, mental oppression or spiritual repression can separate you from His love. (Romans8:35-39)

c. Exile Does Not Mean Extinction

> Daniel 1:3 *Then the king instructed Ashpenaz, the master of his eunuchs, to bring some of the children of Israel and some of the king's descendants and some of the nobles,*

Continuing on the slide that Daniel experienced he was taken captive and in exile where the lifeblood of freedom was robbed away and in an alien land, amid alien people who spoke an alien language he was perhaps at his wit's end – but you know what – exile does not mean extinction; it does not mean the end! In fact, it is the contrary. Are you going through circumstances where you feel you are in exile, where your freedom is curbed, your individuality is diminished, and your creativity is snubbed – you are likely to feel downcast. But Daniel's life gives you hope.

When the tables turn, when the discomfort persists, when the dis-ease resurfaces, do not give in to anxiety, for anxiety does not alleviate, it merely aggravates; do not be discouraged for discouragement does not help advance but it certainly retracts; do not give up for giving up closes all possibilities and it accentuates sure-shot failure; **so** hold on to His word, stand on His promises, and trust Him to make the way and He will. For has He ever spoken and not done it? Has He ever promised and not delivered it? Remember Isaiah 43:16 - *"I am the LORD, who opened a way through the waters, making a dry path through the sea."*

Let me encourage you today. When you trust Him implicitly, you see beyond your circumstances and are filled with peace that is beyond description as the focus shifts from the constraints to the constraints Reliever, from the circumstances to the circumstances Converter, from the adversities to the One who breaks through adversity. Take hold of His promise in Joshua 1: 9 – *"Have I not commanded you? Be strong and courageous. Do not be afraid; do not be discouraged, for the Lord your God will be with you wherever you go."*

My Reflections…

My Response…

My Actions…

PRINCIPLE 26

Acquire the Competencies That Count

> Daniel 1:4 *Young men in whom there was no blemish, but good-looking, gifted in all wisdom, possessing knowledge and quick to understand, who had the ability to serve in the king's palace, and whom they might teach the language and literature of the Chaldeans.*

Daniel's skills panned across a range of areas and he exemplified in multiple fields. He and his friends were the talk-of-the-town. So what competencies did they possess that propelled them to the heights of governance? I would like you to consider a set of competencies that are perhaps key to progress in the corporate den that you are called to serve. I would like to use Daniel and his friends as the standard and consider how you measure up. Here are three distinct sets of competencies that Daniel possessed:

I. Physical Attributes: Appearance And Aptitude

a. No Blemish And Good Looking

In an age where beauty is made with talcum powder, mascara, foundation and a range of external aids that make the heroes of the reel life larger than real life which in several instances are very different from the truth – to stand apart without any makeup is a tough proposition. Recently I watched a clip of a Bollywood actor, considered to be the ladies' man without any makeup, and he looked old, weary with wrinkles on his face and worn out, to say the least. But here were Daniel and his friends, without any colours or makeup; they were without blemish. The old saying, inner beauty is visible on the face is perhaps apt. They were young men without blemish. You have heard the phrase dark and handsome, black beauty; so it's not the colour of the skin or the shades of the skin but the inner beauty that radiates out. The question is, are you without blemish and is the inner beauty surfacing in those outer contours?

b. Wisdom And Knowledge

In an age where most in their peer groups were given to while away time playing and gaming, Daniel and his friends were pursuing a different course. They wouldn't dance to the tune of the world but were engaged and engulfed in a far richer pursuit that kept them updated on the affairs of the land – the political, economic, and social scenarios and they were in a position to go beyond to exercise discretion and convert their knowledge into wisdom. Knowledge and wisdom are two different facets – knowledge is knowing and wisdom is applying the knowledge; where knowledge sets the boundaries of wisdom; wisdom thrives in leveraging the boundaries. The question is do you seek knowledge and wisdom? Is that consciously what you are after? Remember Proverbs 9:10 - *The fear of the LORD is the beginning of wisdom: and the knowledge of the holy is understanding. May the Lord grant you the grace to don the mantle of wisdom and knowledge. We looked at the physical attributes, let's move on to the mental makeup.*

II. Mental Makeup

a. Quick Learner And Finesse

Harvard Business Review defines learning agility as a mindset and corresponding collection of practices that allow leaders to continually develop, grow, and utilize new strategies that will equip them for the increasingly complex problems they face in their organizations. Learning-agile individuals are "continually able to jettison skills, perspectives, and ideas that are no longer relevant, and learn new ones that are," the researchers say. Daniel and his friends were quick learners. They were in a position to take stock of their environments and determine what are those essentials they need to get on top of and which among them they need to imbibe.

Learning quickly calls for an unwavering focus, an insatiable curiosity, and an unending need to learn.

Are you quick at learning? If not, perhaps today is the day to recalibrate yourself and recommit yourself to learning quickly. The illiterate of the 21st century will not be those who cannot read and write, but those who cannot learn, unlearn and relearn said Alvin Toffler and I agree with him. Learning quickly calls for an unwavering focus, an insatiable curiosity, and an unending need to learn. The learning-agile individuals, the Harvard study pointed out, were more socially active, more likely to take charge, more focused, more original, more resilient, and more inclined to challenge the status quo.

Daniel and his friends were not only quick learners but they developed a sense of finesse. Finesse is effortlessness and mastery of a skill. You are so good at it that it flows through with minimal effort and with absolute grace. So these higher-order skills come out of practice and application of the mind. May you have the grace to pick these up and apply them in your contexts.

b. Ability To Serve In A Higher Role

As an OD consultant consulting with many top-notch clients in the country and elsewhere, I often hear clients speaking of hiring fresh blood who have the potential for growth two levels higher. Assessing the potential of individuals is not an easy task for often communication skills tend to cloud the true potential of individuals. The ability to serve in a higher role calls for cognitive capabilities, emotional intelligence, and social skills, along with a range of other competencies.

These are essentially endowed by nature and cultivated by nurture. Daniel and his friends were equipped not merely for the current but for the future role as well. Thus, in my view, they were constantly deepening their learning and honing the skills that enabled them to be better prepared to handle the demands of the role at the next level – to serve at the king's palace. Have you consciously been working on operating at two levels higher? If not, perhaps this is a good day to start.

III. Spiritual Strengths

A recent Harvard study highlighted that the spiritual dimension is perhaps a crucial facet that differentiated truly successful people from not-so-successful ones. Daniel's spirituality was evolved. Let me highlight two aspects of Daniel's spirituality

a. Character Over Class

Daniel and his friends were strong in their intent that they would not compromise their core. It was perhaps convenient to fall in line with the king's order and eat on the king's platter. But Daniel and his friends were aligned differently. Their character was more important than the 'class' considerations of the environment. Do you allow the 'class' issues to override your character? Having flown British Airways several times and enrolled in their frequent flyer programme, I was awarded an upgrade to business class on one of the trips that I was flying with my Managing Director during the times when austerity measures were implemented and all executives were to fly economy. I offered my upgraded ticket to my manager and asked that he flies business instead of me. He blatantly turned the offer down and said you fly business and went on to occupy the economy class. He did not consider it an entitlement to fly business as my boss. That is the character preceding class. Do you allow your character to take precedence over 'class' considerations?

b. Willingness To Derive Strength From Beyond

The source of their strength was the Bread of Heaven. They were keener on the bread of life than the bread of lies. They prioritised the deeper aspects over the surface issues. Do you consider the deeper implications of your surface actions? Perhaps today you need to take a call to derive strength from the bread of heaven and invest in the spiritual dimension.

My Reflections…

My Response…

My Actions…

PRINCIPLE 27

Set the Moral Compass Right

What made Daniel, the ordinary young lad, the extraordinary leader that he became? I would like to share three key lessons that contributed to this transition, in my view.

a. Desisted Defilement

> Daniel 1:8 *But Daniel purposed in his heart that he would not defile himself with the portion of the king's delicacies, nor with the wine which he drank; therefore he requested of the chief of the eunuchs that he might not defile himself.*

In a generation where the lines between right and wrong have blurred, where the appetite for evil has grown leaps and bounds, where the bad is glorified and good subdued, Daniel and his friends desisted defilement. There is an open invitation out there to give vent to your dark side. Some opportunities knock every hour or more to let go of your moral high ground. Some possibilities open up to you on an ongoing basis every moment to compromise your standards.

The availability of opportunities does not mean you have permission to give in, the presence of temptations does not warrant your yielding to them. Much against the world that would have you believe that giving in to your temptations is the way to go forward – the way of the Word is to resist temptation.

The pulls of the universe, the attractions of the cosmos, and the temptations of the world are potent realities. Often they invade you in the subtlest of forms and creep into your eco-system in the most indistinct format. Stay alert, be vigilant, and get sharp-eyed lest you are taken unawares and the snares find their foothold in your thoughts, words, and actions. Ephesians 4:27 admonishes not to give place to the devil. And Matthew 26:41 - "*Watch and pray, lest you enter into temptation. The spirit indeed is* willing, but the flesh *is* weak."

Stick to the moral high ground regardless of the propositions, irrespective of the possibilities and notwithstanding the temptations.

Temptations come in various hues and forms; some are straight forward, easy to tackle while others are rather subtle and challenging to get your fingers around. When you determine in your heart that you will not compromise your principles no matter how alluring the proposition is, when you have decided in your mind that you will not give in to the pulls or pushes of tempting options and when you have yielded your spirit unto His Spirit to lead, guide and secure you, you are likely to stick to the moral high ground regardless of the propositions, irrespective of the possibilities and notwithstanding the temptations.

Often the possibility that you may not be found out or that you may get away with your action could be a powerful motivation to flirt with the option of giving in to the temptation; however, desisting that pull definitively calls for a subscription to a higher code that is not defined by the external circumstances but dictated by the inner conscience that is ignited by the Higher Spirit, informed by the Holy Writ, and inspired by the Higher power. To live with the tug of the conscience is much harder than to live without the advantage that the temptation brings.

1 Corinthians10:13 says, "*No temptation has overtaken you except such as is common to man; but God is* faithful, who will not allow you to be tempted beyond what you are able, but with the temptation will also make the way of escape, that you may be able to bear *it." That is the assurance that you have – that you have a way out organised by God to overcome the temptations that come our way.*

b. Devoted To Prayer

The favour of men comes from God's intervention.

> Daniel 1:9 *Now God had brought Daniel into the favour and goodwill of the chief of the eunuchs.*

Why did God bring Daniel into the favour of others? How did that favour come about?

> Daniel 2:17-18 17 *Then Daniel went to his house, and made the decision known to Hananiah, Mishael, and Azariah, his companions,* 18 *that they might seek mercies from the God of heaven concerning this secret so that Daniel and his companions might not perish with the rest of the wise men of Babylon.*

Daniel was devoted to prayer. Elsewhere we read that Daniel continued to pray even against the orders of the king! The prayers of a lowly saint from the extreme corner of the world have the potency to change his sphere and beyond. For the feeble cries of the saint are heard by the Almighty who is no respecter of people, but is eager to answer the pleas of an earnest heart.

He stops the virulent covid in its path, the ensuing cough and cold in its course and corrosive cancer in its cells and refreshes you with His amazing grace, renews your strength as that of an eagle and rewards you with His mighty presence. Jeremiah 33:3 says, *"Call to Me, and I will answer you, and show you great and mighty things, which you do not know."*

Isaiah 40:31 says, *"But those who wait on the* L*ORD*, *Shall renew their* strength; They shall mount up with wings like eagles, They shall run and not be weary, *They shall walk and not faint."* How is your prayer life? Have you allowed your busy schedules to steal away the solitary time spent with God in prayer?

c. Disposition To Question

> Daniel 2:14,16 [14] *Then with counsel and wisdom Daniel answered Arioch, the captain of the king's guard, who had gone out to kill the wise men of Babylon;* [16] *So Daniel went in and asked the king to give him time, that he might tell the king the interpretation.*

The order to execute the wise men of the land was passed, the king's guard was about their job and Daniel questioned the king's order jeopardising his life and put forth a counter proposition that paved the way for him to be catapulted into the hall of fame. Willingness to question existing practices is a precursor to winning accolades!

As a consultant, my role was to question the assumptions and premises that clients operated on. In a client engagement, a huge Indian MNC's head of strategy was found to be more tactical than strategic. The revelation made to the top leadership called into question the fundamental rationale of the choice of the incumbent, who had a strong pedigree. However, the modification implemented in response to the insight enabled the organisation to develop several times, making forays into numerous business lines and evolving into a business behemoth with holdings in numerous nations across the world.

Develop a questioning mind, evolve a spirit of inquiry, and desist from taking information at face value for the more questions you raise the more you open yourself to possibilities.

My Reflections…

My Response…

My Actions…

PRINCIPLE 28

Unlock the Power Within

The average adult human brain can store an equivalent of 2.5 million gigabytes of digital memory which is called a "petabyte". The human brain possesses about 100 billion neurons with roughly 1 quadrillion, i.e.,1 million billion connections known as synapses, which wire these cells together. Many go through their entire lives without realising what they are truly capable of. Their capabilities go untapped as they do not assess their potential. A diagnostic is perhaps a crucial component of assessing the potential. Once assessed, you are in a position to find ways to unleash the power within. I would like to focus on three key facets that are critical to unlocking the power of the life of Daniel!

a. Testing Is A Pre-Requisite For Towering

> Daniel 1:11-13 [11]*So Daniel said to the steward whom the chief of the eunuchs had set over Daniel, Hananiah, Mishael, and Azariah,* [12]*"Please test your servants for ten days, and let them give us vegetables to eat and water to drink.* [13]*Then let our appearance be examined before you, and the appearance of the young men who eat the portion of the king's delicacies; and as you see fit, so deal with your servants."*

Tests are often viewed as an irritant. Many tend to become unduly anxious when having to be tested. There is a sense of foreboding and hopelessness that surrounds testing for many. This can have devastating consequences for some as they see tests coming up on the horizon. However, we see a completely different picture of Daniel. He asks to be tested. His sense of confidence was so high that he volunteered to be tested.

He recognised that if he were to advance, he would need to subject himself to be tested. It was not a single test – but a series of tests, not a one-day test match but a test series that lasted for 10 days. Not only did he go through a 10-day assessment, but he also passed with flying colours. You know what? Ten Days of Testing leads to 10-fold proficiency – we read in verse 20 - *And in all matters of wisdom and* understanding about which the king examined them, he found them ten times better than all the magicians *and* astrologers who *were* in all his realm.

The assessment was followed up by an interview process. Several IAS aspirants are petrified of the final interviews. But once they clear the final interviews they have the best that the Indian governance offers. What does it tell you? Interviewing is a pre-requisite to scale-up. We find that in (v19). So don't shun interviews, instead scale yourself up to meet the opportunities that open up post the interviews that take you to vistas you never imagined.

b. Uncompromising Standards Yield Coveted Crowns

> **Daniel 2:48** *Then the king promoted Daniel and gave him many great gifts, and he made him ruler over the whole province of Babylon, and chief administrator over all the wise men of Babylon*

Often in the short term living to standards and holding onto scruples is likely to result in misgivings but in the longer term, they bring returns that are credible, lasting and sustainable. There are numerous narratives of people who have chosen to follow their convictions and have reached heights beyond description.

Mr. Raja B. Singh, the senior partner of RK Khanna and associates, a former International Trustee of Gideons International and the founder of the Logos Management Club chose to live by his convictions. In a short documentary with excerpts from his life, Mr. Singh recounts how he chose to follow the way of Jesus and determined he will not compromise his integrity and rewrite the numbers to suit himself or his client. That conviction and pursuant action have stood him in good stead, whereby a client with whom he had a 30% share of the business channelled 100% of the business to his firm, thanks to the integrity demonstrated.

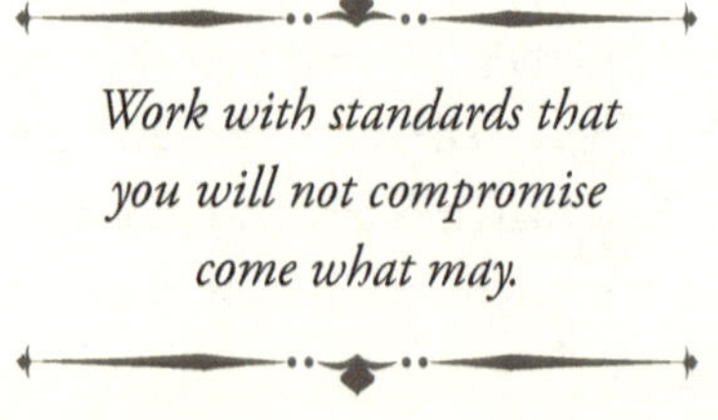

Do you work with standards that you will not compromise come what may? Rest assured that the rewards shall come in their time.

c. Clean Conscience + Veggies Are Better Than A Guilty Conscience + King's Delicacies

> Daniel 1:14-16 [14]*So he consented with them in this matter and tested them ten days.*[15]*And at the end of ten days their features appeared better and fatter in flesh than*

> *all the young men who ate the portion of the king's delicacies.* [16]*Thus the steward took away their portion of delicacies and the wine that they were to drink and gave them vegetables.*

Daniel was not enamoured by the king's delicacies. He was keen to keep his conscience clean. Thus vegan made more sense than non-vegetarian. He was willing to go to significant lengths to keep his conscience unmarred. His decision to keep himself off the non-vegan food was vindicated in that he was found to be significantly better than the rest.

The story of Macbeth comes to mind as you consider a guilty conscience. For the guilt eats into you, erodes your sense of confidence, and erases your comfort taking you often to the edge. The guilt of omission or commission can be equally damning. Doing what you ought not to have done and not doing what you ought to have done can be detrimental to one's sense of bearing.

The interesting thing is you will have people throwing mud at you whether you are guilty or not. But as 1 Peter 3:16 says, Keep a clear conscience before God so that when people throw mud at you, none of it will stick. They'll end up realizing that they're the ones who need a bath. Daniel and his friends chose to have a clear conscience about veggies than a guilty conscience about the delicacies of the king's table. The point to note is that they could have very easily rationalised their actions saying they were at the mercy of the King's orders and therefore they were forced to eat the delicacies. But they were conscious of their conscience and did not want to carry the burden of the guilt.

How often we find people searing their conscience and volitionally choosing the wrong path, pursuing the wrong road and quelling the tug of their conscience. Not so Daniel. He had determined in his heart not to defile himself. How is your conscience? Is it clear or guilty? If it is guilty – get that guilt cleansed today so you, like Daniel, can enjoy a guilt-free conscience.

My Reflections…

My Response…

My Actions…

PRINCIPLE 29

Break the Code of Progress

Everyone desires to progress. The richest multi-billionaire looks for progress and so does the struggling entrepreneur or employee. Progress is ingrained in the DNA and all humanity seeks to move forward to a better place to live, a better position to fill, a better lifestyle – the list is an ever-evolving one. But very few have broken the code to progress. Daniel was one of the legacy builders who had broken the code to progress and here I would place three elements of breaking the code to progress from the life of Daniel.

a. Your Step Of Faith Is Met By God's Hand Of Faithfulness

> Daniel 1:17 *As for these four young men, God gave them knowledge and skill in all literature and wisdom; and Daniel had understanding in all visions and dreams.*

> Daniel 1:8 *But Daniel purposed in his heart that he would not defile himself with the portion of the king's delicacies, nor with the wine which he drank; therefore he requested of the chief of the eunuchs that he might not defile himself.*

The recording of the scriptures is mind-boggling! There is a significant message in the sequence of events that are described. Daniel 1:17 comes after Daniel 1:8. Daniel 1:8 says that he purposed in his heart not to defile himself and followed it up with actions in line with what he had purposed in his heart. When Daniel stepped in faith to honour God, he was met by the Lord of the Heavens extending His hand and honouring Daniel's faithfulness with wisdom and knowledge far beyond anyone else in the entire kingdom.

Often, you end up thinking it is your proficiencies or your efficiencies that propels you forward. The fact is that several others are equally proficient or efficient and in many cases far more proficient or efficient than you are. But you have found your place, which is a testament to the faithfulness of God. It is He who has architected your life journey and it is His faithfulness that charts your way forward.

The key question that you need to ask yourself is: Am I honouring God in every area of my life? Do I give God pre-eminence in the smaller details of my life? Have I stepped in faith to do the right thing?

b. Internal Alignment Is A Pre-Requisite For External Advancement

> Daniel 1:8 *But Daniel purposed in his heart that he would not defile himself with the portion of the king's delicacies, nor with the wine which he drank; therefore he requested of the chief of the eunuchs that he might not defile himself.*

Very often people see the external advancements, the visible progress and the evident achievements, but what is often missed are the underpinning factors that result in the external advancements. The midnight oil that was burnt, the hours that were spent behind the computer screen, the weeks of nurturing the thought, and the months of incubating the idea are all not known to others.

For most, the accolades are visible but not the agonising hours spent behind the scenes. But you know what, the discipline you exercise on your mind and body shall bear fruit one day when everything will fall in place and the world around you will provide a standing ovation for the accomplishments you have achieved. Daniel had aligned himself internally, and determined in his mind, purposed in his heart, and resolved to act on his internal anchor. Your internal anchor paves the way for your external exaltation.

Do you see someone succeed? Do you see someone growing in stature and prominence? If you check with them, they will tell you that they are internally aligned to certain principles, tenets or postulates that they have determined early on that they will not flout. That resolve stands them in good stead to progress. The Tatas as a company has subscribed to five guiding principles that govern their actions says, Shashank Shah. Do you know what these are? 1. Philanthropy 2. Relationship Building 3. Globalisation 4. Innovation and Quality 5. Celebrating Success and Learning from Failures. These principles have ensured that the Tata organisation has grown in stature, size, and substance and is heralded as the company of choice around the globe.

What are the guiding principles that you have aligned to? What are those values that you hold dear to your heart that you will not compromise? If you don't have a set of values that you subscribe to – ensure you take some time to reflect on and agree on a set of principles that you will align yourself to. That will spin the external advancement as never before.

c. Excellence Breeds Excellence – 10x

I would like you to follow the extent of excellence Daniel displayed.

> Daniel 1:17,20 17*As for these four young men, God gave them knowledge and skill in all literature and wisdom; and Daniel had understanding in all visions and dreams.*
>
> 20*And in all matters of wisdom and understanding about which the king examined them, he found them ten times better than all the magicians and astrologers who were in all his realm.*

Knowledge and skill in all literature are to do with a range of subjects. In a day and age of high-end specialisations, this is a very interesting notion of Daniel possessing knowledge and skill across an expansive set of subjects – knowledge is mastery, and to add skill to it would mean he was in a position to leverage that mastery to a higher level that is indicative of excellence – par excellence. To me, the knowledge and skill in literature speak of hindsight.

Additionally, he enjoyed immense wisdom which is essentially a step up of knowledge where the incumbent is in a position to decipher where the knowledge is best used which is essentially insight. Further, he had an understanding of visions and dreams, meaning he was well-versed in envisioning and detailing the vision with foresight.

Daniel 1:20 *"And in all matters of wisdom and understanding about which the king examined them, he found them* ***ten times better*** *than all the magicians and astrologers who were in all his realm."*

Excellence breeds excellence and when you are on the path of excellence, you invariably become better and brighter.

Excellence breeds excellence and when you are on the path of excellence, you invariably become better and brighter.

As leaders carve out their legacies, they are required to nurture hindsight, gain insights, and demonstrate foresight. Are you investing sufficiently in gaining these as Daniel did?

My Reflections…

My Response…

My Actions…

PRINCIPLE 30

Gain Power When You Are Powerless

With the changing panorama, climbing complexities, and challenging demands on an average leader, there are times when you feel powerless. You have done everything by the book, pulled every string, stretched every muscle and still, things don't seem to fall in place. You are likely to feel yourself cornered and completely powerless. In a training session, I was leading a group of international delegates for a client, when my laptop screen blanked out! I had put in a significant amount of work in putting the slides together and I felt completely powerless. Thankfully I had emailed the presentation slides to myself to cover for an eventuality and was able to organize the client's laptop and run the presentation from my mail!

Gaining power when you are powerless, can be a significant challenge. I would like us to examine three key elements from the life of Daniel:

a. Higher The Bar, The Greater The Power

> Daniel 2:9 *If you do not make known the dream to me, there is only one decree for you! For you have agreed to speak lying and corrupt words before me till the time has*

changed. Therefore tell me the dream, and I shall know that you can give me its interpretation."

Daniel 2:46 *Then King Nebuchadnezzar fell on his face, prostrate before Daniel, and commanded that they should present an offering and incense to him.*

Daniel was confounded by a rather difficult situation. The task at hand was akin to being asked to state the questions in the teacher's question paper and answering those questions. The situation was bordering on ridiculous. But that is essentially what was required of Daniel.

The bar was set rather high. Humanly speaking, it was impossible to reach that bar. But Daniel was up to the challenge. Do you know why he was up to the challenge? He was willing to take up the challenge squarely, as he had experienced the divine touch early on where he proved that he was 10 times better than those who had the king's delicacies. Thus he did not see the impossibility of the task but the possibilities of the GOD who was with him to get through the task.

As a consultant to the United Nations, I was required to assess potential UN Resident Coordinators – the secretary general's representatives in various countries of the world. The incumbents were senior diplomats, deputy representatives of the UN, and civil servants from across the world including IAS officers. It was a high-stakes assessment process where the entire assessment was videotaped so that the assessment could be challenged. I was rather intimidated. But you know what? The word of the Lord came powerfully and said, "He that is in you is greater than he that is in the world." Equipped with that word, I regained my confidence and I was part of the entire assessment process for several years across many countries.

Do you have a work situation that seems impossible? Does the bar you encounter seem high? Take heart when you meet a high bar, for the bar ensures you go far. Daniel revealed the dream and the interpretation to the astonishment of King Nebuchadnezzar, and he fell on his face, prostrate before Daniel, and commanded that they should present an offering and incense to him. That is the power of living to the high bar.

When encountered by a rather high bar, don't forget the rewards that come once you meet or surpass the bar.

b. Finding Certainty In The Uncertainty

> Daniel 2:16 *So Daniel went in and asked the king to give him time, that he might tell the king the interpretation.*
> 17 *Then Daniel went to his house, and made the decision known to Hananiah, Mishael, and Azariah, his companions,*

The enormity of the situation is stark. The king had ordered the execution of all wise men and with their lives at stake, all the wise men were perhaps in hiding, hoping to escape the wrath of the king. The tension in the air was perhaps palpable. Uncertainty of the future was at its highest. The possibility of losing one's job, and losing one's life was very high.

Amid that uncertainty Daniel was different; He went in and asked the king to give him time so that he might tell the king the interpretation. And thereafter, he found his friends and devised a strategy to overcome the uncertainty. There are three distinct lessons we learn here:

i. Daniel did not allow the uncertainty to dislocate him. Instead, he was willing to confront the uncertainty in the environment.

ii. Daniel had a set of close confidants that he could trust to devise an effective way forward to overcome the uncertainties.

iii. He exercised enormous faith and took a great risk and that paid him rich dividends.

When encountered by uncertainties, are you willing to confront the uncertainties in the environment? Do you have a set of close friends that you can tap into? Do you exercise faith like Daniel in the face of uncertainties?

c. The Secret Of The Secret Place Of Strength

> Daniel 2:18-19 18 *That they might seek mercies from the God of heaven concerning this secret so that Daniel and his companions might not perish with the rest of the wise men of Babylon.* 19 *Then the secret was revealed to Daniel in a night vision. So Daniel blessed the God of heaven.*

Having bought time from the king, Daniel did not lose time but rushed to the secret place from where he derived his strength. That is the secret of Daniel. He did not consider the perception of the world as a wise man to cloud his vision. He was fully aware of where he drew His strength

Never underestimate the power of the secret place for there lies the true power to unlock the most difficult problems and find answers to the most challenging of questions.

from. Remember that was not the last port of call but his first port of call.

Do you have a secret place where you seek the face of the Almighty God? Do you access the secret place, when you need answers or do you strive to find answers on your own? Never underestimate the power of the secret place for there lies the true power to unlock the most difficult problems and find answers to the most challenging of questions.

My Reflections...

My Response...

My Actions...

PRINCIPLE 31

Attempts to Pull You Down Shall Abound, but You Keep Pushing Forward

As you excel and your work is seen as a benchmark, invariably a section of your peers will not be pleased with the advancement you make. This displeasure in most instances takes the form of dubious practices to discredit you, your work, and what you stand for. While it may be obvious to some within your context, it may not be as evident to others and thus the subtle efforts of your opponents may be under the surface and are likely to go undetected. Daniel experienced a similar situation, but the legacy builder that he was, he turned the situation around. You could potentially be in a similar context. Here below are three learnings from the life of Daniel for you to consider:

1. Plot To Destroy Your Credibility And Question Your Commitment Will Abound

> Daniel 6:4 *So the governors and satraps sought to find some charge against Daniel concerning the kingdom; but they could find no charge or fault, because he was faithful; nor was there any error or fault found in him.*

While your excellence and exemplary work will fetch significant accolades, they shall bring with them a fair number of efforts to discredit you. Plans that could be underway to project you in a bad light are reason enough for you to continue the trajectory of continued brilliance in your work. Insinuations concerning your loyalty to the organization you serve or the cause you subscribe to may make you feel small and insignificant. Here below are three facets of the efforts to pull you down:

a. Your Progress Will Not Be Taken Kindly By Your Peers

> Daniel 6:3-4 3 *Then this Daniel distinguished himself above the governors and satraps, because an excellent spirit was in him; and the king gave thought to setting him over the whole realm.* 4 *So the governors and satraps sought to find some charge against Daniel concerning the kingdom; but they could find no charge or fault, because he was faithful; nor was there any error or fault found in him.*

Daniel's work was impeccable. He went about all aspects of his work astutely with incredible diligence and panache. As an administrator, he was excellent. As a strategist, he was the benchmark. As a statesman, he was miles ahead of his peers. And his peers were not particularly happy with his on-the-job performance. During my early years of work, I had a colleague who would look for ways to put me down and at every opportunity seek to project herself as superior. However, I was blessed with the grace from above to synthesize information, draw inferences, and present it cohesively so that she would reach out to me to crystallize her data and provide my analyses of the information set for her projects. Despite this, she continued to look for ways to pull me down!

When you excel and your excellence is recognized, regarded, and referenced, those not in your league will invariably be disgruntled. They are unlikely to see your contribution to the overall organization, industry, and beyond but will burn with envy at your progress. For in their view, you are merely one among them and the spirit of excellence in you will not be acknowledged. Consequently, they are more than likely to find ways to tear you down.

b. Your Performance Will Be Under A Scanner

Daniel was the cynosure of all his peers. He was being scrutinized on a day-to-day basis. His professional sphere; strategy, tactics and execution, his private life; his interfaces, interactions and intimacies, his value system; his guiding principles, governance and on-the-ground practices – every move of his was monitored, reviewed, and discussed; not a very comfortable position to be in.

As you excel, your performance will be dissected by all, discussed by many, and denounced by some, let that not bother you. When others pay heed to your work, take time to investigate your output and pore over your outcomes. It implies your work is touching the requisite peak performance. Don't let their probes affect you.

c. Your Values Will Be Questioned

> Daniel 6:5 *Then these men said, "We shall not find any charge against this Daniel unless we find it against him concerning the law of his God."*

> Daniel 6:11 *Then these men assembled and found Daniel praying and making supplication before his God.*

A direct outcome of the scrutiny was to question the morals and values of Daniel. When his detractors did not find any holes to punch in his eco-system and he was without a flaw in any facet of his administration or advocacy, they targeted his principles. The intent was not the welfare of the state but the vicious intent of finding a fault that they can dislocate Daniel and halt him in his tracks towards progress.

When others go over your life with a fine-tooth comb and find you blameless, they shall resort to targeting areas that are closest to you – your beliefs, faith, and life choices. Your subscription to a different value system, that is alien to theirs will emerge as a point of contention and will attract significant criticism. Let that not affect you for your excellence at work and your enviable commitment to the organizational goals shall enable you to emerge above board with redoubled status and prominence.

2. Your Punishment Posting Could Be Your Point To Pilot To New Heights

> Daniel 6:16-17 16 *So the king gave the command, and they brought Daniel and cast him into the den of lions. But the king spoke, saying to Daniel, "Your God, whom you serve continually, He will deliver you."* 17 *Then a stone was brought and laid on the mouth of the den, and the king sealed it with his own signet ring and with the signets of his lords, that the purpose concerning Daniel might not be changed.*

Antagonism, when fully grown stops at nothing and seeks blood. Down through the ages, bad blood between individuals, corporates, and nations has resulted in a blood bath. The need to see Daniel ousted ensured that he was posted with lions for the company.

You have heard of senior honest government officials being shunted out to non-lucrative positions as a 'punishment'. Often these punishment positions emerge as a blessing in disguise as it provides an opportunity for the officer to have time for reflection, reorientation, and relaxation, while the area where the officer is posted gets a boost of upliftment due to the meticulous efforts by the officer. Thus, what was meant to be evil is turned into good. Here below are three imperatives as you go through those 'punishment postings' for no fault of yours:

a. Your Plight Will Bring Discomfort To The Powerful

> **Daniel 6:18-20** 18 *Now the king went to his palace and spent the night fasting; and no musicians were brought before him. Also, his sleep went from him.* 19 *Then the king arose very early in the morning and went in haste to the den of lions.* 20 *And when he came to the den, he cried out with a lamenting voice to Daniel.*

Post the order to put Daniel in the den of lions, the king could not take his mind off Daniel. For he was aware of the incredible value Daniel brought the kingdom and the loophole in the system that was leveraged by Daniel's opponents to get him arrested. He perhaps realized his folly in being party to this decision and letting this gross injustice being meted out to Daniel.

Your position ought not to be where you are; you are perhaps wrongfully confined to the position, grade, or scale owing to a flaw in the system and your manager is cognizant of this and is empathic to your situation. Your manager may even attempt to alleviate the situation but to no avail. But don't let their inability to effect any change affect you. During one of the performance evaluation cycles, my manager was able to award me a 20% raise on CTC and was rather apologetic that a higher raise could not be provided. There was a recognition that I merited a higher raise, but owing to certain organizational considerations the increase was not possible. My manager was visibly troubled by this. But remember, a greater glory awaits you as you pass through the lion's den! My CTC increased 24X during the period of service in that organization!

b. Your Prayers Will Be Answered By The All-Powerful

> Daniel 6:20-21 [20]*And when he came to the den, he cried
> out with a lamenting voice to Daniel. The king spoke,
> saying to Daniel, "Daniel, servant of the living God,
> has your God, whom you serve continually, been able
> to deliver you from the lions?"* [21]*Then Daniel said to
> the king, "O king, live forever!* [22]*My God sent His angel
> and shut the lions' mouths so that they have not hurt me
> because I was found innocent before Him; and also, O
> king, I have done no wrong before you."*

Daniel's prayers shut the lion's mouth and kept him safe in the company of hungry lions. The prayers of the righteous are heard and answered no matter how impossible the situation is. Could Daniel have escaped going through the ordeal of the lion's den? He possibly could have. For if God could keep the lion's mouths shut, He certainly could have allowed the king's order to be revoked. But He did not, as Daniel's going into the den and being secured is far more powerful than an order to stop him from being thrown into the den.

On some occasions, going through an ordeal and coming out of it brings greater glory and is thus allowed in your life. A senior corporate executive friend of mine was diagnosed with covid and was on oxygen for several weeks. Everyone lost hope as the doctors had given up the possibility of a revival. But then a breakthrough happened, and he was restored to complete health to the astonishment of all around. That is the power of prayer.

c. Your Provision To Sustain You Has Been Made

> Daniel 6:10 *Now when Daniel knew that the writing was signed, he went home. And in his upper room, with his windows open toward Jerusalem, he knelt down on his knees three times that day, and prayed and gave thanks before his God, as was his custom since early days.*

Daniel having full knowledge of the law prohibiting worship was signed. He went ahead and spent his time in prayer. That prayer perhaps had two components:

i. Protection from immediate harm – sustenance.

ii. Protection over the longer term – sustainability.

In answer to Daniel's prayer, the lion's mouths were shut even before he landed inside the den! Provision for your sustenance and sustainability has been made; so you need to fear no ill.

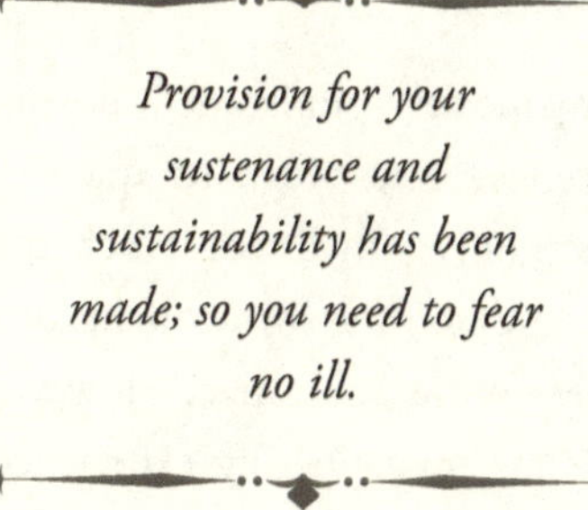

While taking a road trip with the family, I had a foreboding of harm and thus I prayed for God's protection. On the way, the car met with an accident and the car was damaged beyond recognition, but we were spared as a family and came home the next day. The prayers for sustaining us were answered, although the prayer for safety was partially answered – bringing greater glory to God as our lives were spared despite the nasty accident, which brought greater good!

3. Promotion And Prominence Await You As You Progress Beyond Torment

> Genesis 6:23 *Now the king was exceedingly glad for him and commanded that they should take Daniel up out of the den. So Daniel was taken up out of the den, and no injury whatever was found on him, because he believed in his God.*

The torment Daniel went through in the lion's den was perhaps unimaginable. The smell of animals, the dungeon without lights and being branded as an outlaw to the external world were difficult pills to swallow. However, post his vindication the scenario changes completely, and he is honoured beyond comparison. Here below are three distinctions that are guaranteed for the overcomers:

a. Your Innocence Will Be Established

The most damaging issue for anyone on a punishment posting is the establishment of innocence. The pregnant question that takes rounds is, 'is he/she guilty?' Invariably, each one confronted with this question comes to their own conclusions; some more objective and others more subjective. However, being absolved of the charge is an emancipating experience. Being given a clean chit on a charge that you were erroneously implicated is liberating. Daniel was acknowledged as innocent of all charges and that was a vindication. Further, his detractors were thrown into the lion's den, and their fate was sealed. Not only them, but their families were also affected because of their crooked actions.

b. Your Principles Shall Be Eulogized

> Genesis 6:26 *"I make a decree that in every dominion of my kingdom men must tremble and fear before the God of Daniel. For He is the living God, And steadfast forever; His kingdom is the one which shall not be destroyed, And His dominion shall endure to the end".*

Daniel not only was vindicated but was applauded for his stand, and the principles and practices he engaged in. This was perhaps a truly elevating experience. When what he stood for was questioned, ridiculed, and trashed, Daniel did not retaliate. However, the powerful king himself called out and praised Daniel.

You may be ridiculed, mocked, and called names and your holding onto your principles and faith will be questioned, but there will come a day when those who riled you, rebuked you, or revolted against you will be nowhere in the scene, and you will be talked of as having the favour of God.

c. Your Prosperity Is Guaranteed Across Multiple Eras

> **Genesis 6:28** *So this Daniel prospered in the reign of Darius and the reign of Cyrus the Persian.*

Daniel prospered not within the era of a single king but multiple kings. His strength was evident not in one disposition but in multiple dispositions. Thus, he weathered multiple managers and was found to be value-adding across their reigns. When you go through the twists and turns of life, you could either crumble and break or like Daniel stand tall and deliver.

With the right skills and attitude, and applying the principles espoused above you will certainly prosper not merely under a manager but across multiple managers and leave a legacy for generations to come!

My Reflections...

My Response...

My Actions...

Principle Convergence: BEING SALT AND LIGHT

Having considered four stalwarts; a nomad turned father of a nation, a stammerer turned leader, a shepherd turned king, and a captive turned statesman and their lives from ancient history, it is amply clear that you can live a fulfilling life regardless of your background, upbringing, education, or social class. What is particularly noteworthy is that none of them lived flawless lives, and none of them was superhuman; they were all ordinary people who did extraordinary things, each one struggled with their own weaknesses but was made strong, and each had their own predilections yet found their purpose, each had to deal with their own pressures but they found their passion and in the final analyses lived lives that counted and left legacies that stood tall millennia's later. The legacies these men left behind shine through the centuries and call you to take the road they undertook. This essentially is the call that Jesus of Nazareth gave His followers. It perhaps is useful to consider the implications of that call and see how the principles expanded in the earlier pages come alive and converge with that of the assertion of Jesus, the Christ.

> Matthew 5:13-15 13 *"You are the salt of the earth; but if the salt loses its flavour, how shall it be seasoned? It is then good for nothing but to be thrown out and trampled*

> *underfoot by men.* [14]*You are the light of the world. A city that is set on a hill cannot be hidden.* [15]*Nor do they light a lamp and put it under a basket, but on a lampstand, and it gives light to all who are in the house."*

The call given by Jesus is to be salt and light; you are called to be salt and add flavour to your professional and social contexts. How do you add flavour, if you don't have flavour? So the fundamental question is do you bring the flavour that you ought to? There are two distinct flavours that you need to add - the spiritual flavour and the secular relevance of your presence in your professional environment. How do you bring the spiritual flavour into the work context and how do you establish your secular relevance? The spiritual flavour is best brought out by reflecting the spiritual dimension in your conversations, in your conduct, in your deliberations, and in your decisions. Secular relevance is where you consistently add value to your contexts – in terms of professional expertise, strategic foresight, and execution excellence among others. This is where your presence in the room matters. Does your presence matter? For several years during my career, across client contexts, my inputs were sought and valued by clients. I have had senior HR folks calling me to discuss difficult questions and garner insights on people. That is relevant to the context.

The book of Daniel talks about the distinctive spirit of Daniel, and that is something that you cannot contain. It is so powerful and overflowing that it is evident to those who come in contact with you. You do not have to strive – your very presence will add flavour to your place of work. I remember a colleague of over eight years telling me, "I have never seen you get angry even once in all these years." A colleague whom I had to ask to leave owing to performance issues said, "You have been an excellent leader; I could not have done what you have done for me if I was in your shoes." Dear leader, is your life adding significant flavour to your work environment?

The second element is light. Are you truly, genuinely a light in your work context? Light has a dramatic effect on darkness. Are you being the light you are called to be? I would like us to deep dive into these two aspects of being SALT and LIGHT and use SALT and LIGHT as acronyms to cover the essence of what it means to be salt and light.

Let's start with SALT - S of SALT stands for Saturating yourself in the Word of GOD. In Psalms 119:11 - *I have hidden Your word in my heart.* If you are to be the salt of the earth - you need to have the Word of GOD hidden in your heart. What does it mean to have the Word of GOD hidden in your heart? What do you hide away? Gold and diamonds and those that you consider precious; so God's Word is to be precious like gold and diamonds or even more.

The question is, do you assign a precious status to the Word, where you place a high credence to God's Word over anything else? Where His word takes pre-eminence, prominence and precedence over everything else in your life?

Pre-eminence is surpassing all others; where the Word of God is so revered that nothing else takes its place, no matter how compelling the circumstances are. Prominence is influential. Where the Word influences every thought, word, and action and you are so influenced by the Word that you will do nothing else other than what is prescribed by the Word.

Precedence is superseding all else where the Word outweighs all other considerations – personal, social, and financial and the Word reigns supreme in your life. Dear leader, this is a telling question that you need to ask yourself. Is the Word truly supreme in your life?

Not being saturated with His word and expecting to be salt in this world is a contradiction – you can never be the salt in your environment if you are not soaked in the Word – where you allow the Word to read you and speak into your life on the one hand and fill you with the flavour of salt on the other.

The second aspect of hiding His word is that no one can snatch it away. It is treasured and out of reach of circumstances, problems or issues that you face – irrespective of the circumstance that you go through, regardless of the problems you face and the issues you contend with if the Word of God is hidden in your heart, nothing and no one can pluck it out as you have committed it to your memory. Do you take time to memorise the Word? At one point memorising God's Word was such an integral part of the family tradition, but today with the advent of technology I see very few individuals/ families making memorisation a mandate within families.

Psalms 1 says; *"Meditate on His word day and night."* Saturating yourself in the Word means churning the Word through and through until it becomes an integral part of your DNA. This is where at every opportunity in the wakeful day and the sleepy night, the Word of God is the primary reference point, the definitive plumb line and the ever-present yardstick that you use to scan your life against. When you do that, you are on your way to being SALT of the earth.

Let's move on to the A of SALT. A of salt stands for Authenticity. You have an undisputed origin. You are uniquely and wonderfully made. You are no cheap imitation, and God has handcrafted you from a design standpoint, handpicked you from a placement standpoint and handheld you from a providence standpoint, thus you need not attempt to be what you are NOT!

You are to be the Salt of your workplace – and the important thing is that you DON'T need to be sugar!

You are to be the Salt of your workplace, the Salt of your neighbourhood, the Salt in your WhatsApp group and the Salt on social media – and the important thing is that you DON'T need to be sugar! That is not your calling! Do you know what the problem is? Often you are called to be Salt but have lost your authenticity as you attempt to be sugar. You tend to sugarcoat stuff and the salty flavour is lost. My dear legacy builder, don't lose your authenticity. There is an explicit purpose for which you are placed in your workplace, there is a divine intent with which you have been commissioned into your role, and there is a distinct calling on your life that you are purposed to achieve; don't sugarcoat your presence when you are to be the salt.

2 Timothy 2:15 reads, *"Do your best to present yourself to God as one approved, a worker who has no need to be ashamed, rightly handling the word of truth."* You are to show up - unashamed of your calling and be the authentic person you are meant to be; bringing flavour to those that you come in contact with. Bringing flavour means not adopting the

ways of the crowd but being different while blending with the crowd.

How can you be different when you blend with the crowd? Standing for the right, not compromising as others do and not trying hard to fit in but striving to fill in the gaps with your authentic presence. I remember in the early days of my work, we had met together as a team to celebrate and drinks were served. Since we had our President of the APAC region joining us we were given to understand that it would be seen as uncourteous to not drink. I had to decide whether to make a compromise or to stand out. I decided without any hesitation to not compromise, and that was talked about for a long time. So how do you establish your authenticity?

i. Make your mark – always be on target with your deliverables.

ii. Let your presence be felt – don't become the background when in interactions with your colleagues and,

iii. Make a difference – let others miss you when you are not around.

I remember in one of my consulting assignments, we were to deal with GE. This was a high-stakes project and all eyes across the organisation were on this. The team had put together an approach note that was shot down by the client and the team said, "you should have been there - you would have convinced the client." I was away with another equally critical engagement of another client and thus couldn't join in. But I assured the team that I would join in the next call. And sure enough, I joined the next call with the client and post-meeting the team members said, “the client was eating out of your hands.” Be authentic.

Continuing to the L of the Salt**. L stands for Lasting impact;** You know what? You are not to be a flash in the pan, not a one-time occurrence of excellence but a day-by-day, hour-by-hour, moment-by-moment experience of excellence to all those around you. As the salt, you do not have the luxury of being salty at one point and saltless at another instance.

Every interaction is an opportunity to bring a saltish flavour to your environment. It is not a short-term fix but a long-term WAY of LIFE, it is not a role that you play but a lifelong living that you do, it is not a one-time ‘affair’ but an all-time ‘being’. So the ask is to keep the line of sight over the long term and not the short term. Think, breathe and live a life that reflects the core principles that you stand for, that Christ within you is evident in everything that you do.

I remember a colleague who worked with me for several years telling me, “During all these years that I have worked with you, I have never seen you raise your voice. How is it that you can be so calm even in the most difficult of situations?” I of course pointed her to the difference that Jesus made in my life and attributed my behaviour to the work that Jesus has done in my life. The colleague in another context said, “you are the epitome of humility, how are you able to be so humble?”

You know what, those around you will know that you are salt! The Bible says, *“so live a life that is becoming of your standing in Christ.”* Timothy 2:12 says, *“If we endure, we shall also reign with Him, if we deny Him, He also will deny us.”* Being salt is not a sprint event, not a 100 meters dash but a long-distance run where you endure, where you are consistent in your walk, and you continue to bring flavour by the way you interact, interface and intermingle with others. Mark this – your saltiness is noted, documented and discussed by others. So ensure you feed on the Word regularly and refresh yourself consistently such that you make a lasting impact.

Let us move on to the last letter of SALT; T. **T stands for Transforming the environment**. Where Salt is – it should necessarily change the operative environment. Adding salt to food and not experiencing the saltiness in the taste is a contradiction. You are called to be a transformative agent in your work context. The question is when others come in contact with you, do they receive that transforming impact, that therapeutic touch that propels them to seek more opportunities to connect, engage and thrive in the relationship?

The other piece to be mindful of is that SALT does not have to call out that it is salt. Does SALT say, "Hey I am SALT?" No! its presence in itself is so powerful that it blends into the environment in a transformative way and unobtrusively adds flavour. Philippians 4:9 says, *"What you have learned and received and heard and seen in me – practice these things, and the God of peace will be with you."*

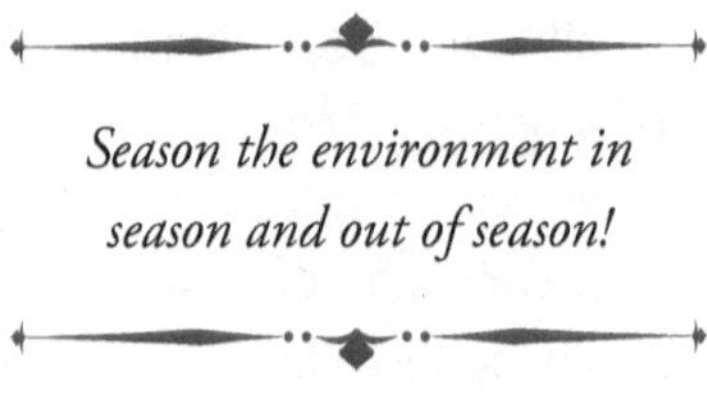

The call is for you to live out being the salt – day in and day out; not seasonally but season the environment in season and out of season! The transformation of the environment could be a time-consuming process. As the salt is stirred in the food, you will perhaps need to stir the environment where you impact the environment positively. That stirring could be painful, uncomfortable and rather demanding, but that permits you to allow the salt to be evident. I remember an occasion when one of my senior consultants who we had hired from a competition was not performing to expectations. There was severe pressure from different parts of the organisation to fire him. It was a tough call, but I stood my ground and as I had hired him I knew his skills-sets, and his context and gave him a long rope. It took him time, but he flowered and won the hearts of clients with his evolved training capability. His underperformance was impacting my performance but being SALT called for me to show grace and the grace then led to him winning the hearts of many.

You are called to be salt and LIGHT. Let us consider LIGHT as an acronym, I would like to consider L of Light. **L stands for Love**. If you are to be an effective light in your context, your light needs to be evident to others by the way you come across to others. The scriptures read, *"you shall know them by their fruits."* (Matthew7:16)

So if you are to be the light, others need to experience you as the light. So how would others experience you as light? By the way you love. Love unconditionally; Love is such a powerful emotion that it cannot be contained. It is pervasive like the light and is evident to all – unconstrained by language. When your thoughts are conceived in love, when your words are clothed in love, and your actions are birthed in love, others will see the love and it cannot be hidden away like the light that is lit is not hidden under the bushel. The love that is real cannot be pushed under the carpet. True love surfaces in day-to-day interactions regardless of multiple efforts by people with personal agendas trying to quell that love.

So the question is what is love? The classical working definition of love is found in 1 Corinthians 13:4-5; *"Love is patient, love is kind. It does not envy, it does not boast, it is not proud. It does not dishonour others, it is not self-seeking, it is not easily angered, and it keeps no record of wrongs."*

Wow, what a description. If you desire to be light in your context, that light needs to show up as love for others. Perhaps this is an opportune time to reflect on how you measure up against these parameters of Love.

Let me help you unravel the components of love. Love is relational and surfaces in varied relationships at work and off work. The prescription reflects a high standard and often may be viewed as idealistic, but may I suggest that indeed the demonstration of love ought to be ideal, so let's deep dive into the anatomy of love.

The first parameter of Love is Patience. '**Love is patient**'. In a world consumed by impatience where everything is needed instantly instant gratification, instant pleasure, instant achievement; love is patient; the instant world invariably resorts to shortcuts and circumvents compliance protocols, whereas love is patient, means forbearance, and often within the work context, this would mean not speaking out of turn, giving a long rope to colleagues and direct reports, giving space to team members to grow and perform. In a world that is driven by numbers, love exhibits patience in dealings with those who don't meet the numbers for 1, 2 or 3 cycles. Do you exercise patience with your colleagues who have not lived up to your expectations? Do you exercise patience with your spouse who has fallen short of delivering the agreed chore yet again? Love brings patience to the fore regardless of compulsions.

The 2nd parameter of **Love is kindness**. Kindness is a virtue that is evidenced as being gentle, mild, tender and pleasant, especially under provocation. It is essentially the opposite of acting bitter, sharp, disagreeable and harsh. Kindness invariably results in positive action of helping others and being considerate towards others which are born out of empathy for others' contexts. Are you considerate towards others? Do you strive to understand others' situations and respond to them in kindness?

Many years ago, while I travelled with a very wealthy person whom I held in high regard, I experienced something significant that has stayed with me since. While in a public place, an urchin came to beg for alms and this rich, highly wealthy person whose net worth perhaps was a million times higher than mine just shooed him away. I went across to the urchin and shared a currency note with him. I was moved with compassion while this wealthy individual refrained from being kind to this boy. Do you bring kindness to others you come in contact with?

The third parameter of Love is **'is not envious'**. Envy is seated in selfishness and jealousy. Envy does not take kindly to others' advancements. On the contrary, love rejoices in the progress of others. True love will not be unhappy about or complain about or desire to dimmish others' achievements or detract from the attainments of others. Proverbs 14:30 says, *"Envy rots the bones."* When you crave what someone else has, rather than being grateful for what God has given, you hurt yourself. The ask is to not envy but love others. Are you envious of your colleagues? Are you burning with hatred of your neighbour's new car or a new house or new job? May you find the strength to replace envy with love.

Moving on to the fourth parameter of love. '**Love does not boast'**. Not boasting essentially means you do not think too highly of yourself; you desist from being egoistic or egocentric. Boasting is tooting your own horn or blowing your trumpet. It does not serve to advance you but rather tends to detract from you. I am not against you sharing your achievements in the right forum with the intent to inspire others. That is enriching. But boasting invariably looks down on people. Often within the work context, you come across people who are waiting for opportunities to pounce on others' good work and claim those to be their own and steal their glory. Love does not seek to glorify yourself but glorify God. In my work tenure, whenever positive feedback came my way or was called out as a goals crosser, I invariably thanked God for His grace and gave credit to my team as appropriate. Do you boast of your strength, your prowess, your proficiency or do you seek to glorify God?

Continuing on the anatomy of love; the fifth parameter, '**Love is not proud'** means you don't move around haughtily as though the entire world revolves around you. There should be no arrogance, no conceit, no vanity; on the contrary, you show up as a humble person, without any pretences. There are different facets of pride: Proud of being the ace, proud of the face, proud of the race, proud of the base, proud of the lace you wear, and proud of the maze you have conquered.

In the consulting role that I served, consultants were doted for carrying a chip on their shoulders, but I was repeatedly known to be humble, I was the go-to person for solutions or interfacing with some of the toughest of clients. Jesus Christ was never proud. We repeatedly read of Him as being humble. Legacy builder, are you Humble?

The sixth parameter of love, '**Love does not dishonour others**', means it does not insult others either in public or in private and does not pull down others such that it affects their sense of self-worth, thus the words used are used with care, restraining from the use of harsh words or sarcastic words that tears down the listener. We all have encountered people who never have a kind word to say about others. The moment they open their mouths, words pour out tearing down others, pulling down others – they don't hesitate to pull down even the most sacred.

One of my colleagues during my official farewell stated that she has never heard me speak harshly against anyone. Let your words be those that build rather than break, construct rather than destruct, enable rather than exasperate, strengthen rather than weaken others. Legacy builder, this is an opportune time to reflect on your life to examine ways you have been slighted by your superiors or in the social context where you were dishonoured for your views, your stand, your background or anything else. Now, perhaps, it is useful to review your life of how you have dishonoured others.

Often as a donor, you come to view yourself to be in a position of higher standing than the one who receives. As a giver, you consider yourself to be on a higher plane than the receiver. The fact is if you don't have a recipient, to whom would you donate? If you don't have a receiver, to whom would you give? Thus, both the donor and the recipient, the giver and the receiver are of equal standing and need to be treated with equal respect and regard. That is love in action. Often you take the recipient and the receivers for granted and treat them differently, with deference to the donor and with disregard to the recipient, with the feeling of awe toward the giver and awfulness toward the receiver. The scriptures say, "Love does not dishonour others." The question is, do you honour all those who come in contact with the same respect? My MD who worked alongside me for several years said, "Pearl treats the MD and the office boy with the same sense of respect and dignity." What a powerful testimony! Do others evidence the same degree of respect from you regardless of their social standing?

Moving onto the seventh parameter of love; '**Love is not self-seeking**' means you do not seek your own benefits at the expense of others. Self-seeking invariably leads to self-serving behaviours and results in dual standards, wherein one has a set of rules for oneself and another set of rules for others. Self-seekers hold the view that 'it's my way or the highway'; self-seekers often trample upon others' rights to uphold their rights, love does not seek their way and position their views as the way forward; people are very sensitive to your moves and quickly see if you are self-seeking or God seeking. In the course of the 360° feedback, I have heard from my manager and multiple other stakeholders that I always place the customers' interests ahead of mine and the organisation's. Are you willing to let others' interests take precedence over your interests?

The eighth descriptor of love; is **'Love is not easily angered'**. Love is not easily angered essentially means that if you are to demonstrate love, you will not have a short fuse. A short fuse invariably leads to an explosion and results in damage that is difficult to rectify. A short fuse shows up as making premature judgments, instant reactions, not thinking through issues clearly, and refusing to provide second chances.

Invariably, most people who have short fuses, repent at leisure. A short fuse is a behaviour and like other behaviours, it is cultivated and the more iterations it has, the higher it gets reinforced until it becomes a part of you and defines your identity. You come to be known to be a man or woman with a short fuse. No one likes a person with a scowl. Everyone likes a person with a smile, even in situations where behind the scowl could be genuine concern and behind the smile could be sharp intent to harm.

All the more reason, therefore, for you who is in pursuit of showing up as loving in your work environment or social contexts, to cultivate the habit of deferring your reaction and responding to situations with love. Giving words to your first reaction in an interface situation invariably results in hasty mistakes that turn out to be costly.

So hold that fuse in check, take a moment to process the information at hand, assimilate the situation fully, clarify and seek more data to arrive at a fuller understanding of the issue and then respond paying attention to your tone of voice, your modulation of voice, and your body language. Communication research indicates that 70% to 93% of what you want to say is non-verbal. Your words may be placatory but your facial contours may reflect a completely different story.

Watch that non-verbal behaviour of yours. It may be a good idea for you to watch yourself when you are genuinely communicating with love to a young baby or your child – how your postures are more open, your eyes are more even, your face breaks out into a smile and your words have zero sarcasm, and are seeded in pure love.

A short fuse is essentially you punishing yourself for someone else's flaws. Doctors say, that as you give vent to your anger, you are inflicting injury to your nervous system. So stay clear of anger and find ways to diffuse it by effective breathing and other workarounds. I know of a star couple who started a venture together. While visiting them at their place she said that if he were to get angry, he would take a 10-km walk to the mountains and come back cool! What mechanism do you have to overcome that anger?

The fact that love is not easily angered points to God's patient love for you. In 2 Peter 3: 9 you read, *"He is patient with you not wanting anyone to perish – but everyone to come to repentance."* If God were to react to your lapses and sins as they deserve, you would have been obliterated a long time ago! But God has been so loving that he does not let his anger be kindled against you. How can you be any different?

Moving onto the last attribute of love; '**Love keeps no record of wrongs**'. As human beings, you are susceptible to committing mistakes, to slip and fall is an integral part of human nature, and to gravitate towards wrong rather than doing right is how you are wired. Where love rules, the past wrongs are not surfaced, accusations are not mounted on the other, love does not keep track of the personal slights that were received at the hands of a colleague or a family member. For several years, I harboured a grudge against an extended family of ours. On reflection, the issue was a non-issue. However, certain members of the family were aggrieved and held a grudge against us. My parents went the extra mile, multiple extra miles to build back the relationship. Despite a volley of insults levelled against them, my parents persevered with much love to win this family over. There came a time when I just let the grudge die and allowed the love to live. It was a liberating experience.

How do you know that you keep no record of wrongs? When there is friction and the voice decibel levels begin to rise, do you find yourself bringing in the issues that went awry between you both in the year of the Lord 2000? If you even allude to what went wrong several years ago that has been discussed, ironed out and moved on, you are trapped in keeping a record of wrongs. Why is keeping a record of wrongs such a dampener in the demonstration of love? The moment you resurrect issues that have been buried and cemented, you are essentially saying that those issues were not buried and that they are still alive in your being and if it is alive in your thought world, they have the potency to come alive in your action world, and once it comes out in the action world, it causes colossal damage. So don't keep a record of wrongs.

The idea is not to let someone repeatedly violate you, but a willingness to allow the past to be the past. We often find people have an axe to grind, but love consciously works to bury the hatchet. Love shows itself in the form of forgiveness.

With that, we move to the I of Light. **I stands for (In)sight**. Light has a telling effect on darkness. When the light is switched on, darkness is dispelled. When the light comes on, darkness goes off; it is a direct perfect correlation. In your work context when you enter a room, when you interact with a colleague or when you share your perspective, your presence, your words, and what you stand for should expel darkness and bring insights to the fore. As a consultant, I have often had clients tell me that the insights I present as part of our consulting engagements are very perceptive and compelling. Early on in my career, the insights I shared with the Chief GM of one of the coal mines enabled him to bridge an estranged relationship with his son who was pursuing his management studies at IIM Ahmedabad. Where did that insight come from? From the LIGHT of God's Word! Let's deep dive into the characteristics of light.

The first characteristic of light is it dispels darkness. Remember John 1: 5 - The light shines in the darkness, and the darkness has not overcome it. The incidence of light expels darkness. Where there is light, darkness does not exist and where darkness exists light cannot exist. In a world that talks of compromises and co-existence here is a telling message. There can be no co-existence between darkness and light. I remember an advertisement hoarding that was placed in the busy central district of Mumbai. It had a girl dressed in skimpy clothing and said, come express your dark side. There is an open invitation at varied points of life to give vent to your dark side, but you are light and you need to expel darkness not embrace it.

The second characteristic of Light is it brings alive inconsistencies that exist in the work environment. As the Consulting Director of a Multi-National Consulting company, I could have sat in the ivory tower and got people in my team or the network to carry out audits. But, I calendared time to carry out audits to ensure whenever inconsistencies surfaced, I addressed them. That is being light. At work, I found an industrious young girl who was in a rut doing administrative work. I saw her potential and highlighted her work to the right people and as part of the leadership team, I influenced others in leadership to promote her to a consulting role and she thrived in that role. So being light calls for bringing to the surface those inconsistencies, and bringing the hidden gems to the fore so that the world acknowledges them and they get a new dimension of life.

The question is are you being a light in your environment? Do others see you as a defining influence or over time have you blended with the darkness?

I like the Complete Jewish Bible translation of John 8:12 which says Yeshua spoke to them again: *"I am the light of the world; whoever follows me will never walk in darkness but will have the light which gives life."* Yeshua expects that you will never walk in darkness. There could be occasions of fights between light and darkness when darkness may seemingly overtake the light. But when darkness takes the upper hand in a situation, don't remain in darkness but move into the light and ensure the shadow of darkness does not pull you down.

The light that you are, drives you to set and sustain a high standard of light.

Finally, true light brings insight – insight is the power or capability to see into any situation in life. Consider Psalm 36:9, *"For with You is the fountain of life; In Your light we see light."* Isn't that wonderful? You see light in His light. That is insight. You understand the inner nature of people, you sense intuitively, and you get to know, and appreciate the not-so-obvious things of life. This insight is given to you supernaturally by God. The Holy Spirit living in you knows all things. He knows the things that God has planned for your life. He knows the direction that your life is supposed to take and He provides you with that supernatural insight. Equipped with that insight, you are in a position to make informed decisions that stand as a beacon in the darkened world. May you continue to be the light that you are called to be.

Turning to G of Light. **G of Light stands for Goodness**. What is goodness? Goodness is the expression of inner sanctity through outer actions. It is pervasive and surfaces in the most corrosive of contexts. Acts 10:38 states, *"Jesus went about doing good."* Jesus, the True Light, went about doing good and you as a reflection of Him can be no different. So continue to do good. Further Galatians 6:10 states, *"So then, as we have the opportunity, let's do what is good toward all men."*

Goodness is not hidden, despite the best efforts to hide it under the carpet, goodness will continue to surface as it cannot be contained. There could be those who out of jealousy attempt to belittle your efforts, underplay your good works or place roadblocks, but the manifestation of goodness is such that it will emerge from the side-lines to the mainstream, from the by-ways to the highway and from obscurity to prominence. Let me highlight how goodness shows up in the environment, as you endeavour to be light:

Generosity Vs. Selfishness

Goodness manifests itself as generosity. Generosity is to do with liberality, magnanimity, benevolence and altruism. As a co-founder of the Giving Pledge, Warren Buffett has committed to donating more than 99% of his wealth to charity during his lifetime or at the time of his death. Selfishness on the other hand is engaged in advancing selfish interests over the interests of others, selfishness focuses on own agenda over the common good.

A good gauge of generosity could be how much you hold back for yourself rather than how much you give. The largesse of the two mites of the widow that Jesus praised, points to this phenomenon. Here is a question to ponder: are you generous? A couple of decades ago one of our office boys lost the roof over his home in a Mumbai devastation. A certain person in the office pulled out Rs. 5000 and gave it to him and he was so grateful, his eyes were moist; 5k at that point was a large sum but this person gave that sum generously and without any expectation or the knowledge of others. One of the neighbours testified at my grandmother's burial that she regularly set aside his share of food, including treats, just like she did for her children in the family. Be generous for generosity will tell a tale for generations to come!

Empathy Vs. Apathy

Empathy is seeing yourself in the emotions and actions of others. Empathy is essential to identify with the suffering of others and wanting to help when others are in need. Being empathic is a powerful expression of goodness such as, I understand how hard this is for you; or, what you're saying makes so much sense to me; or, I wish I had been there with you when that happened; I hear what you're saying, and so on. These communicate that you have their best interests in your mind. Apathy on the other hand is reflected in indifference, detachment, unconcern, and passivity. In your interactions, the lack of concern comes through clearly and the consequences are telling. Do you empathize with others? And does that empathy lead to concrete action on behalf of others? Goodness will ensure empathic interactions.

Humble Confidence Vs. Arrogance

Another way goodness surfaces is through humility laced with confidence. Humility is a clear recognition that others are to be treated as equal and perhaps better than yourself. It is a clear recognition of who you are in the larger scheme of things.

When you observe the cosmic creation of God and the sheer magnificence of His creative genius at work in pulling together millions of galaxies and keeping them in orbit, you recognise how small and insignificant you are. On the other hand, you are to bring the confidence that you are chosen, uniquely crafted with a distinct purpose by the divine hands and that confidence should aid you to not grovel in the dust but stand tall in the knowledge that you are the child of this awesome God!

So while you exercise confidence in your standing, you exercise humility in your status. This is a stark contrast to arrogance which comes up in so many forms. For example, I might turn around and say, "You know who I am? I am the great, great, great-grandson of the poet in the Raja of Travancore's court and the great, great-grandson of the first graduate of Travancore." That is arrogance! While exercising humble confidence arrogance is replaced by assertiveness.

Integrity Vs. Duplicity

Integrity is to do with the alignment of thoughts, emotions, and actions. This is important as integrity underpins consistency of thought, word, and deed. You cannot have actions of integrity if your words and thoughts are not congruent. Starting a life of virtue but living a life of vice is a fundamental contradiction and has no semblance to integrity. It is said of Dr. Billy Graham that he was the same person on and off the pulpit; are your lives consistent? A life of integrity spreads the light to the dark world around such that no one can put it out!

Going further to the H of Light. **H of Light stands for Hope.** We live in a world that is consumed by hopelessness; people everywhere have given in to a sense of despair, despondence and dejection. The pandemic has made it all the more challenging. A few months ago, I had the privilege of being part of the Asia Pacific Regional Conference of World Vision International and the keynote speaker very eloquently painted a poignant picture of the work she does among Mongolian kids who incidentally live in HOLES and their plight is best described in the following poem:

We've lived in holes since childhood

Grew up in darkness

No light in our homes

Tell me mother, why did you give me birth to this world?

We are hungry

For nobody gives us food

There's nothing but singing this song

You can sense the pain and pathos of those kids who are wrought in despair. More than 780,000 people have lost their lives this year; that is a staggering number considering people who died of hunger this year are only a little over 20,000. So what am I saying? Hopelessness is far more devastating than hunger, and it is 39 times more severe as per published statistics.

The number of pink slips that have been given out during this pandemic is pegged at 225 million. Thus, 225 million jobs were lost in 2020 alone. Imagine the number of loans that have been defaulted, the food compromises that were made and the level of hopelessness that exists as the future seems bleak to most. You are called to bring hope to those given to hopelessness. So how do you bring hope where there seems to be no hope?

I remember, during one of our global cost-cutting measures, I was informed by my manager, the MD of India, that we had been asked by the head office to rationalize staff costs. As part of the leadership team, I was to identify people who could be let off. My first response to the MD was, "I am willing to go, as I don't want any of my team members to lose their jobs." When my manager said that was not an option at all, alternately I said that I could forfeit my salary increase for the year and perhaps we can ask other senior leaders in the team to let go of their increases for the year such that we retain the senior resources that were identified to be retrenched. Legacy builder, you are called to be an emissary of hope.

Light at the end of the tunnel is the hope that many pin their lives to, and you are in a significantly advantageous position to bring hope as the light of the world. Why? Isaiah 40:31 says, *"But those who hope in the Lord will renew their strength. They will soar on wings like eagles; they will run and not grow weary, they will walk and not faint."*

So how do you bring hope to a world that is languishing in dark despair? I would like to use the acronym HOPE to drive home simple but powerful ways to light the candle of hope in the darkness.

H of Hope is to Have your eyes fixed on Him, not the situation. Recall Peter's decision to keep his gaze fixed on Jesus in the face of the choppy sea, which helped him stay afloat. Remember to keep your focus set on Him while you, your family, or your coworkers may experience terrifying circumstances, and even though you may feel like there is no hope left and that everything is lost, He will give you the grace you need to go through the ominous circumstances.

O of Hope stands for Operate with an Eternal mindset rather than with an earthly reference point. Often, you could be sucked into a sense of hopelessness because you shift your reference point from the eternal context to the earthly circumstances. When your mindset is anchored on the eternal, you will see beyond the circumstance, to Christ who operates beyond all circumstances.

P of Hope stands for Pivot. Pivot your strengths to your advantage rather than languish in your weaknesses. When you go through those tough challenges, don't waste time on your weaknesses; instead, pivot your strengths, for your strengths will pave way for realizing your promise. For leveraging strengths is far easier to gain mileage during times of uncertainty than working on weaknesses.

E of Hope stands for Enduring the situation with a smile rather than with a scowl. Your response to the darkest night will tell others more about you than when you are at the brightest. The smile amid pain is akin to a sparkling light in the throes of darkness.

Moving on to the last letter of Light – T. **T of Light stands for Transcend**. The injunction to be the light in the darkness has significant ramifications. As individuals and as corporates, there is a crying need to transcend your circumstances and contexts to shine the light in your corners. To transcend is to rise above or go beyond. As light, what are the areas to 'rise above' and 'go beyond'? The following areas are where you are required to rise above:

a. Rise Above Conflict And Ring In Collaboration

It is customary for conflicts to arise when two people gather. Conflict within your professional or personal contexts perhaps is not easily subverted. One useful way around conflict is to put yourself in the shoes of others – this enhances empathy, increases understanding of others' perspectives, and minimizes the impact of landing contrarian views wherein you endeavour to disagree amicably without being disagreeable. The valence of negative emotions is diffused and an objective address of issues at hand ensures a mature dealing of negative information. This approach in turn paves the way for more collaboration. The power of collaboration is perhaps equivalent to the power of ideation.

b. Rise Above Complacency And Usher In Creativity

Today most jobs are automated and success on the job is impingent on curiosity, innovation, and resilience to adapt to new changes. An IBM Global CEO study carried out on 1500 CEOs around the world identified creativity as the most important leadership skill. It is not what one knows that is important; instead, it is what one does with that knowledge that is critical. So the key is to shed complacency, put on the thinking cap and usher in creativity. Remember, God is the creator of the universe, and He is the author of those creative juices that run in human DNA. Tap into that creative genius and let that surface in your work environment. Creativity is where you refuse to look at problems through the traditional lens; instead, bring out-of-the-box thinking to the fore.

Moving on to the areas that you are required to go beyond:

a. Go Beyond The Call Of Duty

Light does not stop being light beyond the "duty hours"; it continues to be the light regardless of the circumstances. Those that stop within the boundaries of established job descriptions invariably set the boundaries of their growth. The call is to go beyond – far beyond the call of duty. A colleague of mine – the head of professional services of one of our global Strategic

Business Units consistently spent close to an hour post any session capturing a debrief and sharing it with all the critical stakeholders. This ensured he was on top of the game and his respect grew across the globe. Over time, he was elevated into the global steering group. Going beyond the call of duty spells excellence and invariably rings in accolades and acclaim.

b. Go Beyond To Walk The Extra Mile

Going the extra mile is a willingness to accede to others' requests, and expending yourself for the sake of others. It is valuing others' requests or pleas and giving credence to them as one's own. My father-in-law consistently takes the extra effort to meet the desires of his interfaces. Whether it is an acquaintance, friend, or grandchildren, he is ever willing to take the trouble to make others happy. There are numerous instances when he would drive to the airport or railway station to pick up friends and family which in turn strikes a positive chord. The power of the extra mile is that it has a ripple effect. It sets in motion a series of positive actions and reactions that the day is filled with positive iterations repeatedly!

c. Go Beyond The Limits

One often sets limits on what one can and cannot do. Most of them are limited by their pasts. Remember, the past is no determiner of the future; when you feel you have reached the breaking point but are willing to push and not give up, you should be on your way to going beyond the limits. When I was called forth to be part of the United Nations Resident Coordinators Assessment Centres in Toronto and other parts of the world, I had butterflies in my tummy. I had serious doubts about my capability to assess the UN Secretary

General's direct line of representatives in various countries. I was strengthened by the Word of God that came alive from Philippians 4:13; *"I Can Do All Things Through Christ Who Strengthens Me."* Empowered by the Word, I took up the task and soon was one of the sought-after assessors in the global team. Any stretch is uncomfortable, but it is the discomfort that paves the way for growth. Remember, the caterpillar goes through significant discomfort, but post the discomfort, it turns into a beautiful butterfly. Go beyond your limits!

You are called to be the salt and light of the world. Would you add three cups of salt to three cups of cooked rice? Definitely not! So even though salt always comes in smaller quantities than rice, while cooking rice it has a significant impact on the outcome. Look at the wall of the space where you are seated. How large is the bulb in the context of the space? Perhaps, a 1:8000 ratio. However, the moment the little light is turned on, the room's darkness disappears completely. You can influence huge events because you are the salt of the earth and the light of the globe.

Sometimes you choose helplessness and opt to go along with the flow rather than stand out for what you believe to be right because you feel overpowered or overwhelmed by the size of the opposing side. Little does not indicate insignificance. You are really important. Your presence ought to make a big difference. Stop waiting to support the majority's position. Even though they may be in the majority, you are the influential minority while they are the unimportant majority. You are the salt of the world, and they are the rice. You are light, and they are the chamber. Create your influence, where ever you are!

My Reflections...

My Response...

My Actions...

Lessons From the Greatest Legacy Builder

I would close with a reference to one of the greatest legacy builders in history; Jesus Christ. His birth spells out key aspects that a legacy-builder needs to take cognisance of, as they endeavour to build their legacies:

1. Voice To The Voiceless

The shepherding community was perhaps the lowest in the rungs of the social hierarchy in those days, as they are now. Jesus' birth was announced to that tier of people who were considered, perhaps, 'outcasts'. And the message of good news, enlivened, energized, and enthused them into action. Luke 2:17 records, *"Now when they had seen Him,* they made widely known the saying which was told them concerning this Child. "What a powerful verse.

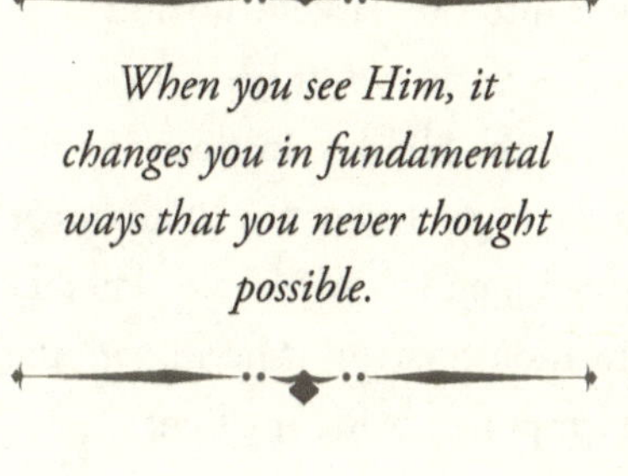

"When they had seen Him," dear leader when you see Him, it changes you in fundamental ways that you never thought possible. It transforms your thinking, it breaks loose those fetters that bind you and propels you forward far beyond your background, your backing, or your baseline. Jesus' birth gave voice to the voiceless. You are called to be the voice to the voiceless, to be the beacon of hope to a world that has lost its hope and to ensure those subjugated under the oppressive shackles of caste, creed or clan are set free so that they find their voice. When they find their voice, they become the ambassadors of their experience.

Proverbs 31:8-9 says, *"Open your mouth for the speechless, in the cause of all who are* appointed to die. *Open your mouth, judge righteously, And plead the cause of the poor and needy."* That is what Christ calls you to do – stand up for the poor and the needy, speak up for the low and lonely, stir up for the upliftment of the marginalised and partisan, and be the voice to the victims of rape, domestic violence, inequality, prejudice and bigotry.

2. Light To The Lightless

Luke 2:9 records, *"Behold, an angel of the Lord stood before them, and the glory of the Lord shone around them."* The advent of Jesus brought light into the darkness physically and metaphorically. Jesus said, "I am the light of the world." His purpose was to usher light into the darkened world. The light of Jesus was evident in the varied works he carried out; whether in restoring eye-sight to the blind or in cleansing the temple, whether in exposing the hypocrisy of the Pharisees or in the dialogue with the learned men in the temple, whether setting new standards of relationships or ushering in the salvation of the soul, Jesus exemplified being the light.

Father Tommy of the Bel Air Hospital in Panchgani lit a light wherein close to 1000 girls from rural areas got educated to become qualified nurses. My wife, Mrs. Priyadarshini John, despite other very lucrative offers, stays in Panchgani to light the candle in the lives of many girls; you are gently reminded to reflect His light in your worlds.

Are you a mini-light in your micro world?

3. Answer To The Answerless

The world is reeling with question after question. There appears to be more questions than answers, more problems than solutions, and more challenges than workarounds. A question by the wise men who followed the star that led them to Bethlehem in Matthew 2:1 *"Where is He who has been born King of the Jews?"* was answered in Jesus. That was perhaps symbolic of the myriad of questions that humanity is contended with – "why do I exist," "Where am I headed," and "What happens after this life on earth"? All of which are to be answered. In John 14:6 Jesus said to him, *"I am the way, and the truth, and the life."* Will you vow to be the answer to life's questions and to point those with questions in life to the answer of all ages and in a sense be the answer to the questions of people around you?

4. Assurance To The Anxious

In the face of uncertainties, fear is the natural reaction and anxiety is invariably what drives most. Fear was the reaction of those who encountered the news of Jesus' birth; be it Mary, the mother of Jesus; the shepherds or the king of the country – all were afraid, maybe for different reasons.

And the message was *"Do not be afraid."* (Luke2:10) We live in a world that is filled with fear; fear of tomorrow, fear of the unknown, fear of unemployment, fear of pay cuts, fear of not being able to keep up, and new acronyms are growing to capture the fears such as FOMO – the Fear Of Missing Out, MOMO – Mystery of Missing out, YOLO - You Only Live Once are mindsets that invade many today. Amid all these crippling fears we have the calm assurance from above "Do not be afraid". You have an opportunity to bring this assurance to your world.

5. Good News To A World Filled With Bad News

We live in a world filled with bad news. You switch on the TV, browse the newspapers, read Twitter, or just dabble in social media, you are confounded consistently with bad news. In the backdrop of all the bad news, there is a distinct counter voice – In Luke 2: verse 10, we have the pronouncement of the good news, *"I bring you good tidings of great joy,"* it says. To a world filled with bad news, the birth of Jesus rings in the good news. What is the good news? That man who is spiritually dead in sin can live! There is life beyond and that life is available to you. The call is that you be a harbinger of that good news in your context and thereby pass on your legacy to those you come in touch with.

My Reflections...

My Response...

My Actions...

www.ingramcontent.com/pod-product-compliance
Lightning Source LLC
LaVergne TN
LVHW041155150826
845673LV00001B/163

* 9 7 9 8 8 8 9 0 9 9 0 2 4 *